Praise for *Power Up Your Dreams*

"If you are feeling stuck, and looking for a way to break out of your perceived mold to go confidently in the direction of what you desire, then *Power Up Your Dreams* is the book for you! Through these pages, you will feel nurtured and empowered by Gloria Carpenter's words and powerful exercises that put you on the fast track to letting your old self go, and allowing your new self to take the driver's seat."

— **Renée Marino, Communication Coach, Best-Selling Author of *Becoming A Master Communicator*, and Mary Delgado in Clint Eastwood's film *Jersey Boys***

"If you have a dream in your heart, you can't give up on yourself. I know firsthand what it feels like to want to quit, but I didn't. *Power Up Your Dreams* will inspire and motivate you to stay true to yourself and go after the life you're longing for!"

— **Marisa Corvo, Recording Artist and 2020 Contestant on *The Voice***

"The best we can do is show up in the world being ourselves and having enough confidence to know that if it's meant to be for us, it will be. 'Just show up and do you!' is my favorite sentence from Gloria Carpenter's *Power Up Your Dreams*. I felt Gloria's smile the entire time I read her inspiring, educational, and uplifting story of following her dreams. She shares many real life and easy-to-do exercises that anyone can do if they are willing to create their own 'dreams do come true' experience."

— **Jodi Suboor, Empowerment Educator and Author of *Healing You With Love***

"Gloria Carpenter is a woman after my own heart. In this amazing book, she shows us how dreams can be achieved if we learn how to envision what we want and picture our future selves achieving it. On some level, this is all intuitive, but too often life gets in our way from letting us achieve what we want. *Power Up Your Dreams* is a powerful reminder that what we need is already inside us, waiting for us to let it out, so we can go from powerless to powerful in so many ways."

— **Tyler R. Tichelaar, PhD and Award-Winning Author of** *Narrow Lives* **and** *The Best Place*

"As a centenarian, I have always stayed active throughout my life and continue to grow and learn. I believe it's important to share the wisdom we have gained to help others along their paths. In *Power Up Your Dreams*, singer Gloria Carpenter does just that, sharing how she transformed from not feeling good enough to being empowered. It's the reason I can sincerely recommend this book to anyone looking to have a more fulfilling and joyful life."

— **Gene Kesselman, 100-Year-Old Author of** *Letters From Grandpa: A Primer for Life*

"Gloria takes you on a wonderful journey of rediscovery that is not to be missed."

— **Brenda Cook, Author of** *The Entrepreneur's Family*

"In this powerful book, Gloria Carpenter weaves her painful story of growing up feeling undeserving and powerless with life lessons learned. Chockfull of golden nuggets, Gloria helps you zero in on what holds you back from realizing your dreams. She then offers a potent game plan to guide you on your path to success. This is a 'must-read' for anyone struggling with a life unfulfilled."

— **Susan Friedmann, CSP, International Bestselling Author of** *Riches in Niches: How to Make it BIG in a small Market*

"Power Up Your Dreams is an uplifting story of a young girl who experienced neglect, abandonment, and lack of self-love at a very young age. Gloria's passion for the arts, music, and theatre helped her reach her goals, but having realized that the external validation is much different than internal validation motivated her to delve deeper, heal, and share her incredible story to inspire others. A must read!"

— Tiffani Patlán, Self-Healing Specialist and Bestselling Author of *Unlocking Your Ability to Heal: Reinvent Your World Mentally, Physically, and Spiritually!*

"Gloria is the opposite of those who want to squash your dreams; she wants to help you build them and see you live your best life. Whether you are a novice in the arena of self-empowerment or a die-hard fan, you will treasure this book."

— Debbi Fuhrman, Actress, Fitness Professional, and Author of *The Joy of Hip Surgery!*

"I fell in love with Gloria's book just from reading the dedication page and her table of contents. Who doesn't want to power up their dreams and make them a reality? Where comparison lurks around every corner, self-doubt becomes your everyday thought pattern. But not anymore! You and I have picked up this book for a reason. There is a stirring in your heart for more. Now is the time to go live out your dreams."

— Crystal Partney, CEO and Founder of Scattering Hope

"In this introspective book, Gloria candidly reveals her very personal experiences and life lessons for the purpose of clearly connecting them to her growth and happiness. Throughout, you can feel her joy and absolute excitement in sharing these strategies to assist others who are on their own personal journey toward living their dreams."

— Lynda Benedetto, Professional Singer and ESL Teacher

"Gloria's book is packed full of great stories, advice, and amazingly helpful tips on how to turn your life from adversity to stepping into your power and creating the best possible life for yourself. A life full of joy, passion, and excitement is waiting for you. But don't wait a lifetime, falling and getting up; read this book and you'll shorten the process and learn from Gloria's wisdom instead. You deserve to live the life of your dreams!"

— **Tom Leegstra, #1 Best-Selling Author of**
The Transformative Power of Travel

"Through her life experiences and the power of example, Gloria Carpenter is truly a shining star who guides you forward into creating your best life! *Power Up Your Dreams* offers a powerful personal growth approach to achieving self-reflection, peace, clarity, love, self-discovery, and true happiness."

— **Terri Rasile Grosso, Professional Life Coach, Music Teacher and Performer, and Transformational Speaker**

"With admirable vulnerability in sharing her personal stories, diligent research that puts the science behind the concepts, and creative easy-to-do everyday tools, Gloria's book inspires us all to start a new chapter in our lives entitled 'The Best is Yet to Come.' *Power Up Your Dreams* is a must-read so you can be inspired and allow your light to shine for a life worth living."

— **Andrea Sooch, Actress, Psychotherapist, and Educator**

"I love this book! Pure nourishment for both my mind and soul. I hope you join me by reading and applying the great exercises in *Power Up Your Dreams* because they provide the power to turn your dreams into the life you truly want."

— **Lorraine Thomson, Life Coach and Author of**
Women Shifting Now

POWER UP YOUR DREAMS!

Moving from Self-Defeat to Self-Belief

GLORIA CARPENTER

AVIVA
PUBLISHING
New York

CONTENTS

DEDICATION

With all my heart, this book is dedicated to those who have endured difficult childhoods, whether they were neglected, abandoned, abused, or mistreated in any way that made them feel unlovable, unworthy, and not good enough. The painful path of feeling undeserving and powerless is about to change as you read this book. My intention is to help guide you back to your innate power so you can get out of your own way and achieve the life of your dreams.

INTRODUCTION

"When you learn, teach."

— Maya Angelou

Let me ask you something: Do you have a dream looming inside of you that you're not pursuing? What made you pick up this book today? Did it have to do with not feeling good enough or deserving enough to make your deepest desires your reality? Is fear holding you back? If you said *yes* or can relate to any of these questions, you're in the right place, and I'm here to help you get from where you are now to where you'd rather be. We all deserve to live our best lives, but sometimes we get in our own way and don't realize it. This book is going to make you more self-aware, which will, in turn, give you more confidence and motivation to attain your deepest desires.

This teaching memoir was conceived and born during a global pandemic—a time when life as we knew it came to a halt and people took a pause from their everyday busy lives. The unexpected coronavirus pandemic was an interruption of normalcy that made most people live in a constant state of fear, worry, anxiety, stress, and uncertainty. It became my own challenge to remain calm and peaceful despite the world's outer chaos. As a working singer who normally performs in front of large crowds, I found my jobs were either cancelled or postponed until the following year. This gave me newfound time to reset, reboot, recharge, and create new projects. It prompted me to delve further into my spiritual practices and gave me the downtime to learn, grow, and expand, along with the desire to share what I know with those around me who were drenched in the darkness.

I felt a calling to occupy my time with doing something beneficial for my soul and to serve others in some way. So I sat down at my computer, and instead of scrolling through my Facebook messages, I opened up a new blank Word document and wrote the title *My Book*. This got me excited and it felt right. Every day, I would take a small chunk of time and write down thoughts and ideas, and I came to realize I had something to say based on my life experiences. If I hadn't chosen show business as my profession, I think I would have enjoyed being a therapist because I love helping people in need and sharing any nuggets of wisdom I've learned to help them out. Within these pages, I'll be sharing bits and pieces of my life story along with a combination of life lessons, practical advice, uplifting and inspirational messages, and references to the concepts of many New Age teachers who have influenced my spiritual growth and, in turn, transformed my life.

"Success comes from the inside out. In order to change what is on the outside, you must first change what is on the inside."

— Idowu Koyenikan

Many people look back at their childhoods with fondness and great memories, but I feel just the opposite when I look back. Growing up, I experienced sadness, disappointment, neglect, and hurt, plus I was incredibly shy, fearful, lonely, and insecure.

A pivotal moment in my life occurred when I was just five years old. I was in the upstairs bathroom of our two-story house. The door was slightly open, so I caught a glimpse of my father rushing down the hall in a huff. I couldn't see what was going on, nor did I realize my heart was about to be broken. "Where are you going, Daddy?" are the only words I remember coming out of my mouth as he angrily stormed past me. I heard the front door slam as I ran down the stairs to investigate. Within seconds, my mother looked at me and uttered words that stayed glued to my mind throughout my childhood. "Your father isn't coming back home, honey." That statement had an immense impact on my inner journey of not feeling lovable, worthy, or good enough because the first man I loved decided not to stick around.

Most of the decisions I made throughout my life were based on how I interpreted that fateful day. I had suddenly become a fatherless daughter, and I chose to believe it was my fault. I have very few memories of my father, but I do remember the love I had for him. One of my fondest recollections was when he came to say goodnight to me while I was still in a crib but old enough to talk. I told him to wait for me to grow up so I could marry him. Little did I know he wouldn't wait. I saw him a few times after my parents separated, but he never gave me his full attention.

During one visit, my father took me and my sister to a park with a beautiful lake that had a small beach area. He was with his girlfriend, and they went off together, leaving us alone to play. My sister, Marlene, being five years older than me, already knew how to swim, but I hadn't learned yet. I watched her expert technique as she joined her friends in the middle of the lake while I walked into the shallow, sandy area. I kept walking until the water was chest level. Tip-toeing very slowly and feeling my way through the water because I could no longer see the bottom, I felt a large rock underneath me and stepped onto it. I had no idea I was on the threshold of the deep area. With one tiny step forward off the rock, I found myself flailing, taking water into my lungs, gasping for air, and panicking because I was drowning. Thankfully, my sister saw me, quickly swam over, grabbed me, and pulled me over to safe ground. She saved my life that day, while my father was nowhere to be found. He showed up a bit later while I was still lying down, recovering. He asked how I was. When I told him I had almost drowned, all he did was ask if I was okay. When I weakly said yes, he didn't stay with me, but walked away with his girlfriend. I had almost died, yet he couldn't hang around!

Because my father decided to leave his kids behind, I concluded that I didn't matter to him and I wasn't worthy of being loved. I didn't know or understand that I deserved better for myself. I became a people pleaser to the core, just searching for the attention I never received as a child. For many decades, I went through life without a sense of self-love, self-respect, or self-belief. I had no confidence in myself, and for decades, I felt lost and alone, floundering through life the best I knew how.

Coming from my very dysfunctional family and having no role models or guidance, I had to learn everything on my own. I didn't realize I was operating with a broken mindset. I didn't know I was feeding my subconscious false stories about myself because that's how I translated my experiences. I never understood that these stories were distorted. Back then, it was my truth, and I believed every disempowering word of it.

The subconscious believes everything you feed it, whether it's good or bad. I didn't realize my thoughts made me feel *less-than*. It took a lifetime of self-discovery to realize I was good enough, worthy, and deserving of all the good stuff. Unknowingly, I was my own worst enemy for a very long time, but my love of music and dance kept me moving forward.

My passion for the arts became my therapy; essentially, my love of show business kept me sane. Music, theater, and dance were my saviors, getting me through internal struggles and pain, and becoming my safe place for expressing myself and feeling fully alive. I was recognized for my talents, which gave me a boost of confidence, but external validation doesn't make up for what you're lacking inside.

While it's true confidence can come from others' praise, it's not the best way to increase your self-esteem because you're giving your power over to others. What really matters is how you feel about yourself.

If you're reading this because you lack inner confidence, it's time to start developing an intrinsic belief in your own worth. It doesn't happen overnight, and you need to become mindful of your self-talk, but each step you take using the techniques in this book will bring you closer to empowerment.

When you have a history of feeling self-defeated, the old feelings sometimes pop up. Whenever you notice yourself slipping back into your old thought patterns, you'll know how to catch yourself and give your subconscious a reality check, reminding yourself that you are good enough *as is*. You *can* have the life of your dreams, and I want you to know that your life matters. *You* matter! You are meant to be here to experience joy and live fully in the uniqueness that is *you*.

> *"You and I possess within ourselves, at every moment of our lives and under all circumstances, the power to transform the quality of our lives."*
>
> — *Werner Erhard*

The person I am today bears little resemblance to the lost child I was growing up. I'm finally in a place of wholeness and peace. My days are filled with joy, fulfillment, and the love of family and friends, but getting here was a very long and bumpy road. The emotional pain I endured as a child transformed itself into lessons, and in retrospect, fueled my growth.

In my younger years, music was my comfort and my therapy. As you probably know, music can be very soothing and can also change your mood. In my youth, singing provoked tears of sadness, but music now brings me joy. It's my happy place, and the sorrow I experienced as a child is gone. I wish this for you too.

How does a shy, quiet, awkward, introverted, self-loathing girl turn into a vibrant, glowing, cheery social being who loves herself and is confident enough to give others advice on coming out of their shells and enjoying life to the fullest? Let's start from the very beginning.

From the time we are born until we are seven years old, our initial programming and subconscious beliefs are being formed. Whatever we experienced during those years is engrained in us, and we take everything in as factual. During these tender years, we can either be nurtured or neglected. Our physical needs must be met and we must also feel safe and loved. Those early days dictate what we require throughout our lives.

According to Dyan Yacoveli's book *The 5 "As"*, the five things the heart craves in life are attention, affection, appreciation, approval, and acceptance—all of which were severely lacking in my childhood. Although my physical needs were met, I never received the proper emotional nourishment to help me make intelligent life decisions. All through grammar school, I found comfort at the homes of my girlfriends whose parents were warm and nurturing. My brother and sister also found friends with welcoming families to help fill the void. We all felt the pinch of being left alone in our immensely broken emotional states.

My parents married young and were nowhere near ready to raise a family, but that's what people did in the 1950s. Neither of them knew themselves very well, nor did they get the chance to explore their career options, dreams, goals, or desires. They simply met, tied the knot, and started cranking out babies. My brother came first, then my sister, then me. I wasn't planned, but despite my parents' relationship being stressed, they decided to bring me into the world.

My mother was a secretary and worked two jobs to support us because our father didn't have the money to take care of us. She did the best she could to provide for us, but her life was very stressful.

My father was musically gifted, fabulously loving, warm, funny, lighthearted, and clearly not ready to take on the role of a father. When I was a toddler, he worked on the railroad during the week and slept all evening, so I rarely got to spend time with him. When he wasn't working, he would usually sit down with his accordion or our out-of-tune piano and immerse himself in music for hours on end.

A few years after my parents' divorce, my father moved to California with his girlfriend. When that relationship ended, he decided to travel like a nomad across the country in his car, going from job to job, never using his passion for music and never finding himself.

He was irresponsible to leave his children behind, but he didn't know any better. In my forties, through conversations with older relatives, I learned my father was always being judged by his family for not having enough money, and he must have never felt good enough. That pattern was handed down to me and my siblings but we were eventually lucky enough to figure it out.

Our parents did what they could with the knowledge and resources they had at the time. I never expressed any kind of anger toward them; rather, I internalized everything that happened, which, in turn, led to a lifetime of disempowering beliefs and self-sabotaging decisions.

I would be remiss if I didn't insert a message to the fathers reading this book. If by any chance you're contemplating a divorce, please let your children know you're still going to be there for them, no matter what happens, and keep your promise. I can tell you from experience that they need you badly. And for any fatherless daughters who can relate to my story, I co-created a song dedicated to you called "What Daddy Didn't See," which you can find on my website: www.PowerUpYourDreams.com.

Some say, "Youth is wasted on the young." I really do wish I knew then what I know now because I did waste a lot of time wandering cluelessly, trying to find my way. I hope reading this book will help you find a more direct route to happiness and fulfillment.

You have no reason to doubt yourself. You were born with greatness within. If no one has told you that before, I'm telling you right now. You are magnificent and have much to offer the world! You may not see it in yourself at this very moment, but I guarantee that as you read through this book, you're going to experience a shift and will come to know the exquisiteness of who you are.

I've come to realize that every single challenge, disappointment, or perceived failure brought me closer to where I needed to be. Lessons were learned, insights were gained, and growth happened. I became strong and more vibrantly alive because of what I endured, and I am grateful for each painful moment along the way.

I now have a beautiful life and continue to sing and dance for a living. Additionally, while writing this book, I decided to become a certified life coach to share my message. I have a peaceful and harmonious life I share with my sweet husband and our crazy cat, and I am blessed with loving and supportive friends and family.

For most of my life, I had no concept of who I was, so I wandered aimlessly, just trying to get by. The woman writing this book today is the new and improved version of myself. My challenges turned out to be learning experiences, and when I was at my lowest points, I mustered the strength to keep going. I figured out what it took to move into a higher state of being and live my days peacefully and purposefully. I became whole, vibrant, and ridiculously happy about the amazing life I created because I finally felt I deserved to have it all. This book will help you fast-track building a life you love. No matter what you endured in your past that caused you to think less of yourself, you are good enough, you are worthy of having it all, and you deserve to have the life of your dreams!

My greatest joy is encouraging people to be their best selves and make use of their innate talents to live their most fulfilling lives. I have a tendency to see the positive attributes in everyone I meet and immediately notice any self-defeating patterns they may have. I'm also naturally in tune with others' gifts—even if they may not recognize them themselves.

We're all unique individuals who are truly special in our own way. No one else alive has our blueprint, and no one else can leave the same imprint on others and our world. By ignoring our inner calling and delaying taking action on whatever burns inside us, we're doing ourselves a disservice and stopping ourselves from living our most fulfilling life.

Your best life begins with acknowledging and believing in yourself. As Lady Gaga sang, "When we're born, we're all superstars." Learn this about yourself and own it!

It may sound simplistic, but I just want to see people being happy doing what they love to do. Maybe it's the hippie generation I witnessed firsthand growing up in the 1960s, but peace, love, and joy are my mojo, and I believe they are the three main factors for a gratifying life. My intention in writing this book is to inspire, encourage, and motivate you to reach your highest potential. We're going to take a look at ways to change your disempowering thoughts and teach you never to give up on yourself or your dreams.

Many of the concepts I learned along the way were taught by New Age thinkers. I'm grateful to those teachers because I am constantly learning and growing. If what I share with you in this book is a new way of thinking for you, I just ask that you keep an open mind and take in whatever concepts resonate with you. By establishing the mind-body-spirit connection and living in balance, your life is guaranteed to change.

The painful path of feeling powerless is about to be obliterated as you read through each chapter. This book is your guide back to your innate power to live your best life and achieve your heart's desires. If anything, I hope my words will make you think about what makes you feel alive and will inspire you to take action to move toward where you want to be.

My heart is full, and my soul is singing joyfully as I envision you transforming your life. You're about to embark on a journey of self-discovery that will help you face your fears head-on and overcome self-limiting beliefs.

You'll notice I reference many inspirational quotes throughout this book. As a lifelong seeker of wisdom, I've always been attracted to sayings that resonate with how I want to live my life. At the beginning of each New Year, I place calendars around my house containing motivational quotes to remind me to stay positive each day. For this reason, I share the ones I think will also inspire and uplift you during our time together.

In my effort to accelerate your journey to where you want to be, I also refer to many of the techniques I've learned over the years from different self-help and inspirational teachers. Similar to a resource guide, I've summarized what each one has taught me, but if you'd like to learn more about them, you can delve deeper into their books and programs.

Additionally, head over to www.PowerUpYourDreams.com right now to grab your free bonuses which accompany this book.

Please note that I am not a therapist, nor am I a scientist. I'm a successful working singer and life coach who helps people build their dreams so they, too, can live a life that they truly love. In this book, I'm sharing my life experiences and the principles, tools, and habits I've acquired along the way that have helped me reach the fullness of who I am today. The information presented consists of basic practices and teachings that have shaped how I view the world and live my life. They've worked for me and for thousands of others. My hope is you'll adapt and adopt some of these lessons into your own life.

The content within is not meant to be medical advice. If you have a chemical imbalance or more severe psychological issue, the techniques described here can be used in conjunction with whatever therapy or medications you may receive from professionals.

To power up your dreams and establish belief in yourself, we're going to discuss the techniques and tools that will assist you in achieving your best life. It's up to you to take the action steps to make these practices your own. As mentioned, the main goal is to help you get out of your own way and allow the magic of self-confidence into your life. Before we go further, let's take a look at what we'll be covering in each chapter.

Chapter 1: We're going to talk about the mindset needed to become fearless. Through my story, you'll see how your life can be transformed by the mere act of taking a risk and leaving your comfort zone. Becoming comfortable with the uncomfortable forces you to grow.

Chapter 2: You're going to take action and discover what it is you really want. Through a series of thought-provoking questions and writing exercises, you're going to envision all aspects of your ideal life. Please take your time with this because we're talking about what truly matters to you. Honor yourself by being thoughtful and detailed in your responses.

Chapter 3: We're going to delve into the innate hidden power within you and talk about your spiritual nature. This topic isn't about religious beliefs but the invisible energy and life force that resides within each of us. It's an essential part of living to your fullest capacity and an aspect of yourself that is often overlooked. We'll also break it down into scientific terms of *vibrations*. We are so much more powerful than we think we are.

Chapter 4: We'll take a look at some tools to help you start believing in yourself and talk about how you can change the distorted stories you tell yourself by becoming mindful of your thoughts, words, and actions. You'll learn about the power of affirmations and living with an attitude of gratitude.

Chapter 5: We'll start developing your self-confidence. We'll focus on practical ways to make you feel ultra-powerful, which in turn will enrich your life. These ways include establishing empowering habits to help you be more productive, centered, and focused and includes lots of "M&Ms." Don't worry; you won't put on weight with these.

Chapter 6: In this chapter, we move into more aspects of becoming self-confident. We'll address the importance of taking care of your body and the advantages of adding music to your day.

Chapter 7: Believe it and you will see it. Please re-read that sentence in case you thought I said "You'll believe it *when* you see it." In this chapter, we'll dig into the topic of visualization and how it can keep you aligned with your intentions.

Chapter 8: We'll talk about the importance of self-improvement and doing your homework to further your skills and abilities. We'll also discuss how perfectionism and procrastination may hold you back.

Chapter 9: Hug yourself right now. We're going to dive into the importance of embracing your uniqueness and staying true to yourself. You'll learn how disempowering it is to compare yourself with others and how collaboration and unity work in your favor.

Chapter 10: We'll explore how it's to your benefit to trust in life and stop worrying about what will happen in the future. We'll also talk about living fully in the present, developing patience, detaching from outcomes, and trusting in the rhyme and reason of the way things happen. Finally, we examine ways to deal with stress when it arises.

Chapter 11: Life doesn't always go the way we want it to. In this chapter, we'll discuss roadblocks, setbacks, challenges, and rejection, and how to handle them by listening to your inner voice. We'll also look into the act of surrendering and how you can be set free to live a peaceful life by practicing forgiveness.

Chapter 12: What's driving you? We'll talk about living intentionally and remaining true to who you are and why you're here. Sometimes your fears get the best of you, so we'll take a more in-depth look at how to deal with fear. We'll also discuss how to make wise decisions, including whether you should quit your day job, which might not align with your overall vision.

Chapter 13: Get ready to rock your world! Through words of inspiration, we'll keep you on track toward having your dream life and living your days joyfully and with purpose. We'll also talk about how you're here to grow and learn, and how lessons can be learned by observing the world around you.

Conclusion: As they say in show biz, "It's a wrap." We'll take a look back at the highlights of what you've learned and leave you with parting words on where to go from here.

Are you excited to begin your journey of self-discovery? Yes? Then I invite you on this journey with me. Let's do this!

Gloria Carpenter

CHAPTER 1

FROM DEPRESSION
TO EXPRESSION

"Remember that wherever your heart is,
there you will find your treasure."

— Paulo Coelho

It's been said that your test is your testimony, and your mess is your message. By sharing our life story, we can help others who may be going through the same things. This book contains pieces of my mess and my message to share with you. I sincerely hope my experiences will touch your life and inspire you to make changes to move forward in your journey. On that note, I'd like to share a little bit of my background because you may draw some parallels to your own life from it.

JUST A SMALL-TOWN GIRL....

I've sung a very popular Journey song from the 1980s, "Don't Stop Believin'," thousands of times as a professional singer. It talks about keeping the faith and holding on to your dreams. I couldn't help thinking about the similarities between this song and my life while writing this book. I was a small-town girl who knew nothing about herself or the world around her. I was living in a lonely world, both externally and internally. I took the train of life going anywhere to find my way and I *never* stopped believing in my dreams, despite the rejections and naysayers. The problem was I stopped believing in myself, and it all started on that fateful day when my home life fell apart.

I grew up in Milford, Connecticut, which was a beach community with a small-town feel. Living near water was wonderful, and I found solace and comfort riding my bike along the water in the sunshine, but my life was far from sunny. Back in the 1960s and '70s, motorcycle gangs and arsonists in my neighborhood always made me feel unsafe. Our neighbors were alcoholics, whom I'd hear shouting and singing at the top of their lungs almost every night. (I'm sure you've heard people singing in a drunken stupor without inhibitions. It's not something you want to hear on a regular basis.) One night, I was up late studying for an exam when I heard someone trying to break into our house. My family was already asleep. I panicked and started screaming. The stranger ran away. Another time, the house across the street was on fire. Watching the embers fly over to our side of the street, I was petrified. I was young, and I felt unprotected, lost, and very fearful.

At the age of nine, I joined a friend at one of her dance classes. I immediately fell in love with dance and begged my mother to put me into dance school so I could learn how to dance my way through life. She was financially struggling and working to support us three kids, but she found a way to make it happen, and I'm forever grateful. I'll never forget my excitement over my first dance recital. Backstage, we all got dressed in our frilly, glittery outfits and were treated to blue eyeshadow and red lipstick to be fully ready for our big moment. It was a simple dance routine to the song "Raindrops Keep Falling on My Head," but for me, it was a grand performance! My nerves were pumping from stepping on a stage for the first time and looking out into an audience full of smiling faces. I was scared, but I knew I wanted more. As the years progressed, I was chosen for lead roles in my high school plays, which is how I discovered I could sing. This began an entirely new on-stage adventure for me.

During those younger years, I had a handful of friends, but my closest was a fun-spirited, talented boy named Ricky. We immediately bonded during second-grade recess when we discovered our mutual love for theater. He also knew at a young age that he wanted to sing, dance, and act. He would put on shows in his garage and ask me to join him. We became inseparable and ended up in the same dance school, in the same community theaters, and played opposite each other in our high school plays.

My first and fondest leading role was playing Dorothy in *The Wizard of Oz*, and Ricky was the Cowardly Lion. We had a blast rehearsing together and continued performing together until our senior year of high school. I loved how fearless and fun he was. After we graduated, he decided he was going to move to New York City and asked me if I wanted to go with him and share an apartment. I told him I'd have to think about it, and I did just that…I thought about it.

Unfortunately, my thoughts were fear-based. I kept asking myself, "Am I good enough to compete with people who are better than me? Can I make a living doing this? Do I have what it takes?" My internal answers to all of those questions were a resounding "no," so instead of pursuing my passions, I ended up going to college for a degree in elementary education. I figured teaching would be a secure job and I'd have my summers off. Ironically, I'm not very good with disciplining kids and had a horrific time student teaching. It was the furthest thing from an enjoyable experience. I intrinsically knew it wasn't the right path for me, but it felt safe.

During the early 1980s, teaching jobs were hard to find, and I was unable to secure a regular one. In retrospect, I think this was life's way of pushing me in the right direction. I got married soon after college and worked a few day jobs, but then I decided to go back to my musical theater roots, so I ventured into community theater again. Dancing in the kitchen in my tap shoes felt right.

I did a few shows at a professional theater in Bridgeport, Connecticut, called the Downtown Cabaret Theater, where I received my first paycheck for doing what I love. It was only $25 per show, but it was a sign there might be a chance of making some money singing and dancing.

The other performers became my family and were fully committed to their passions. Some were Equity performers who took the train in from New York City (NYC) and made their living doing shows. (Equity is the actors' union.) During rehearsals, we were all in *a zone* and loving every moment of what we were doing. I had forgotten what that was like, but it felt like home to me.

My marriage was short-lived, and we ended up separating within two years. My theater family knew I was going through a rough time, so they encouraged me to start auditioning in NYC. I still wasn't feeling ultra-confident, but my peers acknowledged my abilities, which bolstered me. One of them told me about an upcoming audition for a cruise ship position as a singer-dancer.

Going to New York City scared the hell out of me. In the past, any time I mentioned wanting to go to NYC, my mother would say it was a dangerous place. I had only been there two times as a teenager, once with Ricky and once with a group of high school friends. I had never traveled there on my own, and I didn't know the lay of the land. But this time, I followed my heart and knew it was finally time to create my new life. I faced my fears and took on the challenge.

On the day of my audition, I boarded an Amtrak train from Milford to Grand Central Station and went on my very first solo adventure. I had on my favorite blue dress and was wearing my three-inch heel, Capezio dance shoes. No one had told me to bring a change of shoes for my first walking expedition in New York, and I ended up going from 42nd Street on the East Side down to 18th Street on the West Side.

If you're unfamiliar with the streets of Manhattan, let's just say it was a *really* long walk. My feet were killing me, but I didn't care. I was mesmerized by the vastness and intense bustle and energy around me, and the sights, sounds, and smells kept me captivated.

When I finally arrived, I discovered it was a private audition and not a casting call. They were looking for an immediate replacement for someone who was leaving. I sang a couple of songs, did a few dance steps, and was hired on the spot!

From that day on, I made a vow to keep chasing after my dreams and not to settle for something that I didn't enjoy.

It was also a memorable day because after the audition, one of the casting people asked which subway line I was taking to get back to Grand Central. I innocently replied, "There are subways here?" Everyone laughed, and I got a briefing on how the subways work. My feet were happy, and I was overjoyed to be starting a whole new life.

This was my first lesson on becoming fearless. I took a chance, showed up, and got the job. When the ship gig ended, I became relentless in auditioning for different types of shows and ended up getting hired in a show band that performed six nights a week, five shows a night, including two musical theater variety shows and three dance sets...all for a whopping $50 per night. Once again, I was making money doing what I loved.

One night while we were on the road, a New York talent manager approached me. He walked up to me after the show and said, "I think you're terrific and unique. I'd love to work with you. Here's my card." It was the first time someone of significance acknowledged my skills. He said he could get me work doing solo gigs, but at the time, I had become comfortable with this particular band and didn't have the confidence to venture out on my own.

I held on to his card for a very long time, but I never called him because I didn't want to leave my comfort zone—plus, subconsciously I didn't believe in myself. I didn't realize it at the time, but my fears and lack of self-worth were still getting the best of me.

Through my experiences, I've found that living in fear keeps us from living our most fulfilling lives and wastes our time if we're not mindful of why we're not moving full steam ahead.

Be honest with yourself right now. Do you live in fear? What's holding you back from achieving your ideal life?

"The transformative process is our job, so that we are not ruled by fear but by love."

— Ram Dass

Much like Dorothy in *The Wizard of Oz*, it's only fitting that it took me a lifetime of experiences to realize the answers were always inside of me. And yes, I can tell you there's no place like home. Once I became fearless, I was able to gain more and more confidence. Had I been armed with the information in this book, my bumpy path would have been smoothly paved and the rocks would have been pebbles. I would have known how to deal with my situations and to have full confidence that I was on the right track. Would have, could have…but that's not how life goes. You live, you learn, and if you feel the call, you share what you know.

"You gain strength, courage, and confidence by every experience in which you really stop to look fear in the face. You must do the thing you cannot do."

— Eleanor Roosevelt

I encourage you to live fearlessly and leave your comfort zone if need be. Live from a sense of strength and courage, and be brave when it comes to pursuing your dreams. If you have a dream you really want to pursue and you aren't moving in that direction, you need to discover and acknowledge what's holding you back. Here are a few questions about your self-beliefs to ask yourself while you're still here at point A before you embark on a new journey to point B: Do you feel unworthy or undeserving of having it all? Are you struggling with the sense that you aren't good enough, talented enough, or skilled enough to get to where you want to be? If so, your subconscious fears are probably getting in your way.

Most people fall into the *not-enough* mindset and base their truth on past experiences that have become engrained in their subconscious as fact. It's up to you to figure out exactly what is keeping you from taking action in moving toward what you want. Chances are you have some emotional clearing out to do.

If your inner child is as damaged as mine was, it's in your best interest to look into releasing that energy as soon as possible. You need to operate from an open vessel, not one full of old wounds. To do that, you have to become aware of what's going on inside you. In this book, you're going to look inward and find out what's holding you back. So, are you ready to get rid of your fears and self-limiting beliefs? If so, it's time to get proactive. Think about this next set of questions and what they bring up in you.

If you truly believed in yourself and lived fearlessly, how would you live your life? What would you do differently? How would your life change? How would it feel?

Now that you have an idea of what a fear-free life would look and feel like, let's find out what will truly make you happy and fulfilled and fine tune it.

CHAPTER 2

WHAT LIGHTS YOU UP?

*"Follow your bliss and the Universe will open doors
for you where there were only walls."*

— *Joseph Campbell*

As a professional singer in love with what I do, I feel compelled to ask you these questions: What makes your heart sing? What makes you feel alive? What excites you? What are you passionate about? What are you naturally good at?

Your answers equate to your purpose and your reason for being. You were born with innate gifts to use and share with the world, and once you discover your true passions, you'll have a clearer idea of what it's going to take to get you from where you are now to where you want to be.

I knew the answers to these questions while I was still wearing pigtails. At that time, my mother insisted I get to bed by 9 p.m., but once a week, she made an exception because she knew I had a favorite TV show called *Million Dollar Movie* that played old movies from the 1930s and 1940s. It was there and then, sitting in front of our dial-controlled, black and white TV that I realized what I wanted to do with my life.

I was mesmerized by the Busby Berkeley musical numbers involving chorus girls in glitzy costumes singing and dancing to intricately designed choreography that had them moving into different geometrical patterns. They were filmed at different angles showing their various formations and were captured from above in magical kaleidoscope fashion.

I was also enthralled by the water ballet choreography in Esther Williams films and by the musicals with legendary dancers like Gene Kelly and Fred Astaire. But it was the movie *42ⁿᵈ Street* that solidified my desire to be in show business. It's the story of a girl named Peggy from the suburbs who moves to New York City with the hopes of getting on Broadway. She gets a break when a director notices her talent and adds her to the chorus of his newest musical, only to have the lead character sidelined with an injury. Peggy gets chosen to take over her role. The girl with stars in her eyes had instantly become a Broadway success. I felt a strong connection with that young, naive girl, and I felt compelled to follow the dream that she and these other amazing performers placed in my heart. I just had no idea how to get there.

Even though I knew I was drawn to music and the theater, and I intuitively knew it was my calling, I had no idea I would lose my power when I experienced an emotional downturn. As previously mentioned, my parents got divorced when I was ten. My father moved to California with his girlfriend. The night he came to say goodbye, I pretended I was asleep because I couldn't face the pain of losing him.

From that point on, my life changed. I lost my zest and was an emotional mess. The only solace I found was in music and my continuing involvement with theater and dance classes. For months on end, I cried uncontrollably and played guitar to accompany myself as I sang sad songs to help soothe the pain.

I eventually swept all of the emotional baggage and feelings of abandonment under the rug, but it took me most of my life to realize I was going through life feeling unworthy and scared.

The one thing I was forced to develop during my childhood, however, was self-reliance. I had to learn how to live on my own, with no money, no mentors, and no guidance. I did the best I could, but I now know if I had believed in myself, I would have had a more peaceful, productive, and successful journey.

> *"You are not given a dream unless you have the capacity to fulfill it."*
>
> *— Jack Canfield*

When you genuinely have a dream in your heart, it becomes a burning desire inside of you. You feel driven to make it your reality, and it's a flame that can't be blown out until you decide you no longer want it lit. It's a constant presence gnawing at the fiber of your being. Successful people know exactly what they want. They've visualized what it will be like when it actually happens. They have vision and focus. They can see it and feel it in their bones. They figure out how to get there and take the necessary action steps. They stay in tune with who they are and what they want, and they eventually achieve their goals—only to start new ventures.

Many people discover their talents and desires when they're younger, but many others are still searching for their true calling. Wherever you are on your path, it's time to get to know yourself better and define what you want. American psychologist Abraham Maslow said, "What a man can be, he must be. This need we call self-actualization."

To find meaning and purpose, self-awareness is one of the keys. You need to know what makes you feel fully alive. This world provides us with a wealth of contrast so we can pick and choose what feels right to us. Do you know yourself well enough to state your dreams emphatically? Have you given thought to why you want to move forward from where you are now? What does it mean to have a fulfilling life? What will make you truly happy? It's time to reassess (or assess, as the case may be) what you crave.

We're going to go through a series of writing exercises that will help you clarify your dreams. I encourage you to get a notebook or start a new document on your computer to act as your journal. Title it: *My Journey of Self-Discovery*.

Take your time as you move through each exercise. It may take you a few days to find clarity, but please don't skip these action steps or move on to the next chapter until you've completed everything. I'm here to guide you, but you have to put in the work. Believe me, it will help transform your life, but you must be willing to uncover what's holding you back.

EXERCISE 1: BRINGING IN THE NEW BY RELEASING THE OLD

To heal your past, you must understand it. You need to become self-aware and figure out why you're in your own way. The reality of your childhood isn't as important as the perceptions you place on it. This first exercise will help you process your old beliefs and transform them.

Step 1: In your notebook or in a blank document, write, "Young (insert your name)." Now list anything you went through that made you feel undeserving, unworthy, and unloved. Write down what you felt about any incidents that caused you to stop loving yourself. This may not be easy if you had a difficult childhood, but it's important to face your inner demons head on. There's a broken part of you that needs to be brought out in the open in order to heal. You may be an adult now, but there's an inner child within you that causes you to doubt yourself and live in fear, and which stops you from living a happy life. Take your time with this because it's a necessary part of clearing a path to growth. Don't move on to Step 2 until you've sufficiently unloaded all your old baggage.

Step 2: Acknowledge that these old thoughts still exist inside you and are the reason you live in a disempowered state. Growing up, you inadvertently created false stories about yourself, and your sub-conscious believed those stories. I'm going to repeat this because you need to hear it again. You created lies about yourself based on how you felt at any given time. You have always been worthy, de-serving, and lovable, but something happened that made you feel the opposite. You internalized your thoughts and reactions to your circumstances and started believing them, but the truth is, you were damaged and scarred by not knowing how to process what was happening. You didn't deserve to be treated the way you were, and you now need to accept that what's done is done, and that the pureness and beauty of who you are is ready to emerge and blossom.

Step 3: Write a letter to your inner child from your adult perspective. Write down any self-limiting thoughts you may have had and address them with self-affirming statements. Preface it by writing, "Dear (insert your name), I'm here to tell you that (insert any non-serving belief you wish to release from your subconscious, along with a statement saying the opposite)." For example, if it were me, I'd write, "Dear Gloria, I'm here to tell you that you didn't deserve to be abandoned and that you were worthy of having loving parents. It wasn't your fault. You are deserving, worthy, and lovable and always have been."

Step 4: Acknowledge that you are the owner of your own thoughts. No one else does your thinking for you. This is a powerful thought in and of itself. You, and you alone, control what you think. There will be more on this topic later, but for now, all you need to do is accept that you can control your life through your thought patterns. Repeat after me, "I get to choose my thoughts!" Repeat. Repeat again.

Step 5: On a separate piece of paper or in a new document, write down the title "The New (insert your name)." Now write down five to ten statements about your new self who is free from emotional blocks. Start with the words "I am." For instance, some positive statements that worked for me were, "I am good enough. I am worthy and deserving of having my best life. I am strong and ready to show up courageously in the world." Make sure what you write inspires and empowers you to become your most confident, powerful, strong, and happy self. Let go of past mistakes and forgive yourself because you didn't know any better. You were doing the best you could with the knowledge you had at the time.

Step 6: When you're done writing statements of strength, print them out and look at them daily. Read them out loud. Believe them and *feel* them down to your core. This exercise will clear the path to freely expressing yourself confidently in the world. We're going to talk more in-depth about the power of affirmations in Chapter 4, but for now, start entertaining new thoughts about yourself and how amazing you are!

EXERCISE 2: FOLLOW YOUR JOY

Oprah Winfrey said, "Passion is energy. Feel the power that comes from focusing on what excites you." Following your joy is a pathway to an exceptionally fulfilling life. When you're excited about doing something you love, you get into a zone and time disappears. Whatever that *something* is for you is your *raison d'être (reason for being)*, otherwise known as your purpose. In this exercise, you're going to get in touch with your gifts and abilities. ***Respect your talents and your life will be more meaningful.***

The following exercise will help you pin down what you truly want to do in this lifetime.

In your journal, write down these thought-provoking questions and take your time answering them.

1.   What makes you feel alive and in the moment?

2.   What activities or hobbies put you in a zone where time doesn't exist?

3.   What brings you joy?

4.   What are you naturally good at?

5.   What would you be doing if money wasn't an issue?

6.   Who are you when you're at your best and feeling aligned with life?

EXERCISE 3: CREATE YOUR WISH LIST

On a new blank page, draw three columns and title them: Be, Do, Have. Then start creating a list of everything you want to be, do, and have. (If you'd like a template to work from, you can grab a free copy at www.PowerUpYourDreams.com.) Take all facets of your life into consideration including your dreams, your profession, your relationships, your health and fitness, your financial life, your personal growth, your social life, and travel. Write down the details of the life you envision. I encourage you to find some quiet time when you won't have any interruptions and to take your time with this. This is a very important step in the process of transformation because you can't get somewhere if you don't know where you're going.

When you're done writing your list, take a look at the following questions, courtesy of Vishen Lakhiani of the Mindvalley community. These might prompt you to add more items to your list and lead you to your deeper purpose and desires.

1.   What do you want to experience?

2.   How do you want to grow and develop yourself?

3.   How do you want to contribute to the world?

(Note: In the resources section in the back of this book, you can find a link to Vishen's in-depth video explanation of each of these questions.)

Once you're in tune with your gifts, it's in your best interest to use your talents to give back to the world. Giving to others brings purpose to ourselves and others. As Blake Mycoskie, one of the guest sharks on the show *Shark Tank* and co-founder of the company Madefor, puts it, "The more you give, the more you live!"

Once you've completed your list and answered the three questions, take some time to absorb what you wrote. Soak it all in and imagine what your life would look like if you obtained all you wished for. My guess is you'll be feeling pretty darn fantastic about the prospect of having, being, and doing everything you feel called to do.

You've just created your ideal vision and have more clarity about your true desires. Give yourself a pat on the back for doing the work and refer to your wish list often to stay focused on what you really want.

It's now time to *Power Up* your dreams. How do we do that? It's such an easy solution, but many people don't take the time to explore this necessary option. It's a matter of tapping into your inner world. In the next chapter, we're going to delve into aligning yourself with your true purpose and desires. Just like your laptop, you need to plug in and connect daily to your power source. Once you turn your computer off at night, you need to plug the power back in to get it up and running again in the morning. That power is essential for it to work at full capacity. Similarly, you need to dip into a power center to obtain all the things on your wish list. With your innermost desires and dreams close at hand, it's time to dig a little bit deeper to discover your true self.

CHAPTER 3

WHO ARE YOU REALLY?

"The most beautiful experience we can have is the mysterious. It is the fundamental emotion which stands at the cradle of true art and true science."

— Albert Einstein

Are you aware of how powerful you are? Do you know that everything you've ever needed and all of the answers to your deepest questions are always available at a moment's notice? To give more power and energy to your dreams, there's a secret that most people either don't know or simply don't take the time to investigate. It's hidden but requires such a simple process to discover. You see, your true power is inside of you! Everything you need to live a full and happy life resides within, and all you need to do is take a few minutes out of your day to connect to that inner energy. You have the capacity to be so much more than you are now if you develop a strong belief in yourself powered by your hidden energy source.

I'm sure you've heard about the mind-body-spirit connection. In this chapter, we're going to focus on what I consider the most important of the three. It's your true source of power and what drives you forward feeling motivated, guided, and focused upon what's important to you. Whether you call it your soul, your spirit, or your Higher Self, it's a huge part of who you are. It's the door to inspiration, focus, and creativity. By definition, the word *inspire* means *in-spirit*. We are spiritual beings at the core, and the best way to attain the wholeness and beauty of life is to tap into that energy. It's your life force, and the word *force* equates to power!

I'd like to preface this section by saying that this is a topic that can profoundly change your life. This isn't about organized religion, but instead has to do with your inner world and the invisible energy inside you. All I'm asking is that you read it with an open mind because it can alter your life in ways you could never imagine.

> *"Religion, science, and spirituality help us make sense of the world. Life without at least one of them is a lonely and confusing place."*
>
> — Naval Ravikant

We're all raised in families with their own beliefs about spirituality, so we've either been conditioned to believe in a power greater than ourselves or we haven't. Many people adopt the practices and convictions they grow up with. That wasn't the case with me, so I'd like to share my religious and spiritual background and how I landed where I am now.

My first weird and frightening moment happened at a very young age. My mother and my grandparents were dressed up in their finest outfits and took me with them to a barren-looking white cement building down the street from our house. It was unlike any place I'd ever seen, and it had an eerie feeling to it. When we walked inside, we were welcomed by a musty smell and rows of wooden benches. My grandfather started walking ahead of us into the main room while my mother took my hand and said, "We have to go upstairs, honey." The balcony had a special section for the women, though my mother didn't tell me why. After we sat down on the uncomfortable benches, all I could see below me were men wearing shawls and head coverings and bobbing their heads up and down while speaking strangely.

I was scared. What was happening? Why were we upstairs and not bobbing our heads too? Why did we have to be so quiet and not make any noise? Why wasn't anyone telling me what was going on? All these thoughts ran through my head but I was too afraid to ask, so I never got answers. I didn't know anything about religion and certainly had no idea that we were in an Orthodox synagogue.

I was born Jewish and most of my extended family adhered to the traditions. But in my house, we didn't practice anything other than half-baked versions of certain customs and holidays. No one explained anything to me, and I was forced to take part in rituals that made no sense. On Yom Kippur, the holiest day of the Jewish year, considered the day of atonement when all sins are forgiven, we were forced to fast from morning to night. It was my least favorite Jewish holiday because I hated not being able to eat, and when I questioned my mother about why we had to do it, she just said, "Because that's what we do."

It was the same at Chanukah when we had to light a candle every night for eight days. I grew up in a Catholic neighborhood, so all my friends had cool Christmas trees adorned in garland and tinsel. Why couldn't we have one of those? Why were we lighting candles instead?

Eventually, we visited my aunt and uncle, who kept a Kosher home. They explained the whole story. They told me about some of the rituals of Judaism after I put the dishes away in the wrong cabinets because I didn't know that Orthodox people separate their *meat dishes* from their *dairy dishes*.

I never did get over wanting a Christmas tree. One year, I couldn't take it anymore, so I went outside, gathered up some branches, planted them in a pot with soil from my backyard, brought it into the house, and decorated it with tinsel and garland. I topped it with a Jewish star and told my mother it was a Chanukah bush!

I continued to adorn the rest of the living room with garland and silver tinsel that glistened when the sun hit it. It made me happy, and my mother didn't seem to mind. It wasn't until my grandparents came over for Christmas dinner that all hell broke loose. (Yes, our family celebrated Chanukah on Christmas Day. Try to figure that one out.) My grandmother told my mother all the Christmas decorations had to be taken down, including my beloved Chanukah bush. I was angry, disappointed, frustrated, and very, very sad. If my mother didn't care at all before my grandparents' visit, why did everything have to change all of a sudden? It didn't seem fair or just.

I started off on a bad foot with religion, but I wasn't ready to give up exploring other possibilities. Next up on the religion train was becoming part of a Baptist youth group. My sister had joined initially, and then a few of my friends invited me to join them. I was immediately hooked by the love and acceptance I felt from everyone there, and other than my involvement with dancing and theater, I finally felt like I fit in somewhere.

I began reading the New Testament and fell in love with the stories and the words that spoke to me in a profound way. There were no strange customs to adhere to like my experiences with Judaism; instead, I observed a feeling of being something other than my physical self. I got wrapped up in that sensation and started preaching to my friends and *witnessing* on the streets by handing out pamphlets that said there was only one way to God.

This all happened as I was transitioning from grammar school to high school. I was a speaker for my eighth grade graduation and was so engulfed in the born-again movement that I added a sermon-style segment based on Bible verses that I was forced to modify. I kept in a couple of Gospel verses and the importance of loving each other because I felt that was the main theme.

I didn't know what it meant to love myself, and I subconsciously needed to feel loved because I hadn't during my childhood, so the loving concepts in the Bible resonated with me. I was instantly labeled as a *Jesus Freak* by my fellow classmates in freshman year of high school, but I didn't care. It felt right to me. I even got into the Jews for Jesus movement for a minute.

Things changed during those high school years. Religion took a backseat to the drama and music departments. I had a new and more intense love for the arts, which filled me, but I realized I had no self-confidence, and my internal world was being unmasked. I felt alone, even though I had friends. At sixteen, I learned how to drive and had to pay for car insurance to use my mother's old car, which she graciously gave me, so I stopped taking dance classes and got a job.

I fell into a self-sabotaging habit of binge eating whenever I felt alone or depressed, and I gained a lot of weight. I couldn't look in the mirror without feeling disgusted. I didn't love myself and felt unlovable. I even had suicidal thoughts. I tried to kill myself with aspirin, but only took enough to put me to sleep for a little while and woke up still feeling miserable. I didn't tell anyone about my depression and continued to keep my smiley mask on. Fortunately, in senior year, I became friends with a girl who didn't judge me and with whom I could be myself. She was one of the popular girls in school, so I was accepted into her group of happy, confident, lovable girls.

I based my self-love on what others thought of me back then instead of recognizing my own self-worth. I did manage to slowly pull myself out of my funk, but religion was the last thing on my mind because I didn't feel like I had any direct connection to a power greater than me. I still felt like I was traveling through life on my own without the help of anyone or any unseen force. I continued to self-sabotage and lived in a state of self-defeat and not feeling good enough for decades. ***It never occurred to me that the love I needed most was self-love.***

Everything changed in my late forties when I went through a very painful breakup of a long-term relationship and felt lost. I started taking yoga classes to help me feel grounded. At the end of each session, the instructor had us lay on the floor on our backs in a *savasana* pose and just rest in the stillness. This quiet time prompted me to investigate what was really going on in my inner world, and I began asking deeper questions about my behavior, thoughts, and actions. This process led me to book an appointment with a therapist who said I had unresolved abandonment issues from my childhood.

It took almost fifty years, but I finally discovered I was going through life disempowered because of my childhood! With that knowledge, I started reading books on healing inner wounds and soaked up every word—they all seemed to be describing my life.

I was damaged and needed to find a way to heal my inner child, so I started looking for helpful books and came across a website for *The Fatherless Daughter Project.* I immediately ordered the book of the same name, written by Denna Babul, the creator of the Fatherless Daughter Movement. She had gone through similar life experiences growing up without a father, and I was floored to read how all of my decisions, actions, and behaviors were based on the one simple act of my father walking away.

I then went to Codependents Anonymous meetings, where I heard other stories like mine and learned about the Twelve-Step recovery program. I didn't know most of the steps were based on acknowledging a Higher Power and surrendering to God.

For instance, Step Two says, "We came to believe that a power greater than ourselves could restore us to sanity." And Step Three is: "We made a decision to turn our will and lives over to the care of God as we understood God."

In an instant, I had come full circle back to my spirituality, but this time, it wasn't a religion. There were no customs to follow, no preaching, no reason for anyone to feel God was unattainable. This was a direct path to God—from my heart to that Invisible Energy. It was the beginning of my new spiritual journey. I was learning to surrender and trust in my connection to my Higher Self. In effect, I was starting to plug in to my spiritual life, which was powering up my entire existence.

Although I didn't associate with any religions, I found that I was most aligned with the teachings of the Baha'i faith, Hinduism, and the Unity Church, which honor all religions. Any religious doctrines that purported love and unity as their major themes were the ones that resonated most deeply with me. I concluded that there are bits of wisdom in all faiths, and that all roads lead to an all-knowing *force* greater than us. I believe this energy is always looking to expand itself through us, or as Oprah Winfrey puts it, "You are the channel and God does a livestream through you."

This energy has many labels. Whether you call it God, the Universe, the Creator, the Divine, the Quantum Field, Source Energy, Life Force, Consciousness, Infinite Intelligence, Conscious Awareness, Higher Power, your Higher Self, Higher Guidance, the Soul, Entelechy (coined by Aristotle), or however you define that which is unseen, it is the formless energy that dwells within us and is all around us. It's all that is, and we are each a part of it. I've come to agree with the French philosopher Pierre Teilhard de Chardin's statement: "We are not human beings having a spiritual experience; we are spiritual beings having a human experience." I live my days knowing there is greatness inside me and inside each of us. We are limitless and powerful, and it's important for you, dear reader, to know this about yourself.

"You have to grow from the inside out. None can teach you; none can make you spiritual. There is no other teacher but your own soul."

— *Swami Vivekananda*

WHAT DOES THIS ALL HAVE TO DO WITH CHASING YOUR DREAMS?

You're probably wondering why I'm bringing up spirituality in a book about pursuing your dreams and living your fullest potential. It's because your power source comes from within. To live a peaceful, purposeful, meaningful, and fulfilling life, it's important to establish a connection with your inner world and discover your internal spiritual space. There's a *higher intelligence* inside you that knows what's best for you. This is the way to *power up*. All you need to do is take the time to plug in daily. To power something up, you have to turn something on or plug something in, right? Once you hook up to that hidden internal power source, you'll find that you'll be happier, more centered and focused, and more productive. People ask me why I'm always so positive and happy. It's because I tap into my spiritual world. Doing so will do the same for you.

How do you do that? How do you find that connection? One of the easiest ways is through meditation, which is simply an act of closing your eyes, quieting your mind, and looking inward. Meditation comes in many forms. I'll discuss it more in a later chapter, but for now, I invite you to try something. Take a few minutes to stop reading and close your eyes; take a few deep breaths and just sit in the quiet and stillness. Concentrate on the breath going in and out of your nose. Your thoughts will come and go, but just notice them as they float through your mind. Acknowledge them, let them go, and return to your breath. If you're a busy person who simply doesn't have the time, you'll be glad you did this for yourself because it's a quick way to recharge and reboot. Ready? Set the timer on your phone for five minutes. Close your eyes, breathe, be still....

Welcome back. How did that feel? Are you a little bit calmer? Less anxious? Feeling more peaceful? That was just a tiny taste of the amazing effects you can get from such a simple process. ***Sitting in silence is an elixir for your soul and your sanity.*** The more you meditate, the more you'll come to know and experience a power and energy greater than yourself, which is always available to you. All you need to do is acknowledge that it's there and plug into it a few minutes each day. It is so simple, yet so effective!

NOT BUYING IT?

We're so much more than we think we are. At the core, we are energetic, vibrational beings who emanate from an energy source of infinite intelligence. This magnificent unseen and powerful field of energy from which we all originate can't fully be comprehended by our human brains, nor can it be seen with our human eyes, but we have access to it at any time by the mere act of being aware that it exists. Think about it. We're just specks in one galaxy among 200 billion galaxies. We didn't create ourselves. Yes, our parents had something to do with it, but I'm talking about the miracle of how we automatically transformed from zygotes into full-fledged human beings. We don't breathe ourselves, and our body knows exactly how to operate without us telling it what to do. There's something intangible and miraculous at work here, but if this premise is too *out there* for you, let's get back to discussing the material world as we see it and look at a different perspective on who you really are.

For the non-believers and my atheist friends, let's take the scientific approach. It's understood among scientists and in physics that everything in the universe is made up of vibrational energy—and that means everything, including humans. In the words of Albert Einstein, "Energy cannot be created or destroyed; it can only be changed from one form to another. Everything in life is vibration."

Physics explains that we are basically experiencing our consciousness, which we interpret through our five senses. The vibrations of our bodies move so fast that we think we're solid beings, but we're not. An ever-present electromagnetic energy is released from the sun and travels in waves, such as ultraviolet light, radio, TV, heat, x-rays, microwaves, and others. This energy also occurs inside of us and fluctuates with different thoughts and feelings. Electrical signals multiply like a wave to thousands of neurons, which fire, leading to thought formation. Thoughts lead to emotions, and our feelings and emotions are electromagnetic.

Let's take a look at the findings of David Hawkins' in-depth research on this topic. Hawkins was a scientist, physician, and clinician in the field of consciousness research who received prestigious acknowledgments and lectured extensively about his discoveries. He conducted a twenty-year study using a unique muscle-testing method where he used calibrations to determine how emotions and state of mind correspond to levels of consciousness. From his studies, he wrote his first groundbreaking book *Power Vs. Force* and created a *Map of Consciousness* that lays out how lower energies keep us disempowered. He showed how a person's log level, which is the measurable energy level in their magnetic field, increased as that person experienced more positive emotions. Using a numerical scale from 20 to 1,000, Hawkins scored the person's results based on levels of consciousness, which correlated to the person's emotional state. Listed from low to high, those levels were: shame, guilt, apathy, grief, fear, desire, anger, pride, courage, neutrality, willingness, acceptance, reason, love, joy, peace, and enlightenment. Hawkins concluded that, "We are all born with a level of consciousness, an energetic frequency within the vast field of consciousness."

One of my main influences, the late Wayne Dyer, introduced David Hawkins to the world via one of his PBS specials. Dyer was quick to point out some of Hawkins' studies. Here are two that Dyer shared in a blog that I found pretty mind-blowing.

- One individual who lives and vibrates to the energy of optimism and a willingness to be non-judgmental of others will counterbalance the negativity of 90,000 individuals who calibrate at the lower weakening levels.

- One individual who lives and vibrates to the energy of pure love and reverence for all life will counterbalance the negativity of 750,000 individuals who calibrate at the lower weakening levels.

During some of Dyer's talks, he invited an audience member on stage for an experiment to prove that every thought you have can be assessed as to whether it strengthens or weakens you. With the volunteer, he conducted a simple muscle test. He'd have them hold their arm out to the side and ask them questions. Then he'd attempt to push their arm down while asking them to resist. First, he asked them to think of something that was true, like their name and where they were from, and asked, "Is that the truth?" The resistance at that point was strong, so he would then ask them to lie about their name, and then asked them the same question, "Is that the truth?" If the person said yes, their resistance was weak. This muscle test was also valid when Dyer asked the person to think of something where they felt shamed, angered, or wanted revenge. The resistance to his push was always weak, but when Dyer gave the direction to think of something or someone they loved, the resistance was strong.

Just for fun, try this out on a friend. This can be done for any thought that elicits an emotional reaction. If they ask you why it's happening, you can answer, "Because we're vibrational beings."

Similar to David Hawkins' chart, yet very different in application, Christine Gail, author of *Unleash Your Rising*, created a story approach to the states we experience throughout life. She designed a self-leadership blueprint called *Your Story of Intention*, which makes us aware of disempowering states we may live in either consciously or unconsciously. Through her techniques, people can move from disempowering states to a state of reverence for their lives. The higher state of third story reverence includes the gifts of the spirit: peace, love, and joy. These higher frequency states are the core of who we are. She teaches that underneath it all, as we release the disempowering perceptions of our stories, we see we are, in fact, whole and complete, made in God's image.

Hawkins was just one among the many scientists who delved into the science of discovering who we really are. According to an informative article by Arjun Walia on the Collective Evolution website, titled "Nothing Is Solid and Everything Is Energy: Scientists Explain the World of Quantum Physics," what we perceive as our physical material world is really not physical or material at all. This has been proven time and time again by multiple Nobel Prize winners.

One of those winners was Danish physicist Niels Bohr, who said, "If quantum mechanics hasn't profoundly shocked you, you haven't understood it yet. Everything we call real is made of things that cannot be regarded as real."

Nikola Tesla, the inventor and engineer who discovered and patented the rotating magnetic field, and is best known for his contributions to the design of the modern alternating current electricity supply systems, was quoted as saying, "If you want to know the secrets of the universe, think in terms of energy, frequency, and vibration."

Modern-day physicists have also developed a new theory of how the universe operates called string theory. Brian Greene, a well-respected, contemporary physicist, has been educating people about this theory in user-friendly language. He basically suggests that below the atomic and sub-atomic particles lies something else. He refers to them as *dancing filaments of energy*, which are tiny filaments vibrating at different frequencies.

As you can see, science points to the fact that you are a vibrational being and not what you see in the mirror. Whether through belief in your spiritual nature or by accepting the scientific approach of our vibrational nature, embrace your own power and use it to take action steps to move toward where you want to be. If you're not convinced you are more than your body and mind, I'd like you to interpret the rest of this book to mean: Live from your heart and listen to your inner voice, which holds your truths and guides you.

Speaking of taking action, let's go one step further than we did in the last chapter. This time, you're going to do the exercise from the heart and with your eyes closed.

Tune out the world right now; close your eyes; take a few deep, cleansing breaths; and ask yourself, "What are my most deep-rooted desires?" Sit with that question and listen for the answers that come to you. Keep asking and keep listening. If something pops up that's not already on your wish list, add it.

In conclusion, you are more powerful than you think you are. You're magical and magnificent and here to shine brightly doing what you love. To do that, you'll need to get out of your own way. In the next chapter, we move on to a practical approach to helping yourself. We'll find out how those non-stop thoughts of yours are affecting your life and how you can make them work in your favor.

CHAPTER 4

CHOOSE YOUR
THOUGHTS WISELY

"Thoughts become things...choose the good ones!"

— *Mike Dooley*

Freshly-divorced and in my mid-twenties, I had a newfound desire to be the best *me* I could be. That is when I came across a self-help teacher named Anthony Robbins, known today as Tony Robbins. Back then, most people knew him as the enthusiastic, energetic guy who had people walking over hot coals. Some thought he was crazy, but I found his teachings intriguing and extremely motivational. I never went to any of his seminars or walked over the burning coals, but I was an avid follower of his words and still own the original 1986 copy of his book *Unlimited Power*, which had instantly inspired me to push myself forward. It was the first time I heard someone say we have the power to change our lives by choosing the thoughts we think. Just the thought that we get to create our own stories and alter our lives by merely changing our mindset was mind-boggling! It made me feel more optimistic and hopeful that I could be the successful person I wanted to be.

As enthused as I was, I had no idea that my subconscious beliefs about myself were getting in the way. I denied the existence of self-defeating thoughts or self-sabotage, and yet that was the space I lived in. I thought I believed in myself because I knew what I loved to do and had learned through experience that I could make money doing it. But that wasn't enough to propel me full throttle to my highest potential. I needed to believe in myself and not just in my dreams. That was the one thought that was missing from the equation of my success.

Years later, I came across a book called *Consciously Creating Circumstances* by George Winslow Plummer. It was published in 1935 and later republished in 1993. The concepts within reinforced and solidified the message I had learned from Robbins, that our thoughts create our reality. At that point, I was finally ready to incorporate this notion and accept that I had the power to intentionally choose a new perspective. This time around, I was ready to receive the full meaning of those words, and it became apparent to me that I needed to think better thoughts about myself and dream bigger dreams. This was also the first time I'd heard of a spiritual connection to a universal energy, and as you know from the last chapter, I believe that is where our true power resides.

In my case, I had a lot of reprogramming to do. Can you recall your very first memory? How far back can you go? Mine took place at the age of two. My mother needed to go back to work, so my parents decided to enroll me in a day care center while they left my older brother and sister at home to take care of themselves. I vividly remember my mother carrying me on her shoulder, walking into a pink house, and being greeted by a stocky older woman with a dirty apron on. In an instant, I was handed over to this unfamiliar woman and watched my mother walk away. I didn't know what was going on, but I remember my deep and exhausting cry when the door closed.

I'm sure my mother left me with comforting parting words, including that she'd be back, but it didn't matter. I was left alone in a strange place with a strange woman. I was handed over to someone I didn't know, and I felt unwanted and unloved. This experience became ingrained in my subconscious and was the beginning of a lifetime of thinking I wasn't lovable or deserving of love. It was at the root of my self-doubt and lack of self-worth.

For seven years, Monday through Friday, I was dropped off at this pink house run by Mama Flood. The other kids became my surrogate family, but some of them weren't kind to me. I was bullied a few times and had no one to come to my rescue. One night at the kids' dinner table, which was in a room away from the adults, we were served cooked spinach, and I hated it. We were told we couldn't leave the table until we ate everything on our plate, but this green stuff tasted nasty. All of the other kids were gobbling it up and started leaving the table, but two of them decided they would torture me. One plugged my nose and forced my mouth open while the other one rammed the spinach into my mouth. It was traumatizing, and nobody was around to witness it. I didn't say anything because I was afraid of what else these pranksters would do to me if they knew I had tattled. I felt alone, even though I was among other kids, but fortunately, Mama had a house full of cats; those furry animals became my best friends. They loved unconditionally and were always available when I needed solace.

On countless weekends, my mother took day trips with her sister and left me overnight at Mama's house. A few of those times, I didn't get to talk to my mother before she left on her weekend vacation, and she'd pick me up after work on Monday night. My father was supposed to come visit me, but he rarely showed up.

On one visitation day when he actually made an appearance, he brought along a catalogue and told me I could get anything I wanted out of it. I didn't want to order the higher-priced items because I didn't feel worthy of receiving expensive gifts. Even though he told me not to worry about it, I didn't ask for the pricey Barbie Dollhouse I wanted but chose a doll that was cheaper.

We grew up on S&H Green Stamps, and my mother always shopped at thrift stores and wholesale outlets. Every Saturday, we'd take a trip to a local Entenmann's outlet where there were different colored dots to tell you what percentage you got off of the price. My mother would bring home boxes of cakes and pies from the red-dot specials rack strung tightly together. Unfortunately, this started my lifelong sugar junkie, emotional eater pattern, which caused my body to change and was yet another hurdle to cross.

I had no idea what the word *abundance* meant because poverty was all I knew. I was taught that *money doesn't grow on trees* and we couldn't put on the heat or air-conditioning unless we really needed to. We were encouraged to save our pennies and had jars filled with coins. I carried this thought pattern throughout most of my life. Fortunately, I eventually learned I needed to revamp how I processed the thought of money. My older and wiser self knows this is a bountiful universe, and it's our birthright that abundance flows freely to us so we can enjoy our lives while giving back to others.

I also learned that the life energy that breathes us also wants us to be rich, so we should welcome prosperity with open arms and feel worthy of receiving it all. We are deserving of all good things, but we have to allow them into our life and not push them away like I did whenever I was offered something that cost more. The story about living *hand-to-mouth* was engrained in me from an early age. Not until I started flipping that story to one of abundance did I start attracting wealth into my life.

SELF-BELIEF BEGINS BY CHANGING YOUR STORY

You are the only one who can control your thoughts, which means you get to choose your reality. We touched upon this previously, but it's important to truly absorb this message, so it bears repeating. Our thoughts are powerful! Tell yourself a new story and your life will change. Replace your fear of not being good enough with a solid belief that you are more than good enough.

Henry Ford said, "Whether you think you can or you think you can't, you're right." Our thoughts can either serve us or hold us back—disempowering us. What stories are you telling yourself?

Most people are conditioned by their childhood and past experiences, and due to their internal beliefs about what happened, they believe they're not *enough*. Because of this, they lack self-confidence, self-respect, and self-love. They live in fear of failure, so they don't take risks or put themselves out there. They're their own worst critics, and they search for perfection. They compare themselves to others who seem to have it all, not really knowing what the real story is behind someone else's successes.

Does any of this sound familiar to you? It all rang true for me because I had created my own sad belief about myself...one that made me unhappy and affected every decision I made that had anything to do with feeling deserving. Due to my abandonment issues, I told myself I wasn't good enough, but I was feeding myself a lie. I was indeed good enough, and I *was* deserving. The truth was my father made the choice to leave because he didn't know any better. He wasn't ready to be a parent, and that had nothing to do with who I was. All it took to change my paradigm (my subconscious thought pattern) was recognizing that I had misinterpreted my childhood experiences and hurt myself in the process. To get to that point, I found a couple of New Age teachers who talked about this subject in detail, and I started assimilating their findings and teachings into my life. Below I'll discuss a few of the noteworthy enlightenment guides I suggest you check out if you're unfamiliar with their teachings.

Wayne Dyer was one of the most popular self-help authors and motivational speakers of our time. His teachings transformed the way I think and live. Whenever I need a dose of inspiration, I turn to one of his more than forty books. One book is fittingly titled *Change Your Thoughts, Change Your Life: Living the Wisdom of the Tao*. Pulling on the concept of the Tao, or rather that invisible energy of what is all around us and inside of us, Dyer encourages us to live authentically, fully, and with conviction. In his bestseller, *The Power of Intention*, the subtitle of the book states his popular quote, "Change the Way You Look at Things and Things You Look at Will Change." Another of my favorite Dyer books is *10 Secrets to Success and Inner Peace*, which highlights many of the lessons I've adapted to my own life because they help to keep me even-keeled. Fundamentally, the more we become aware that our thoughts create our emotions, and our emotions create our actions, the more we learn how to make decisions that benefit us rather than keep us in a negative state.

Many of the most effective teachers and coaches who help people transform their lives tend to share the crucial knowledge that everything starts with a thought. Louise Hay, founder of Hay House and another one of my early influences, also talks about changing your thinking. She is known for saying, "A belief is just a thought and a thought can be changed." She's best-known for her groundbreaking book *You Can Heal Your Life*, which claims all forms of disease, or as she puts it, *dis-ease*, are caused by our thoughts. Many people have been healed or comforted by her words. Another of her quotes is, "The most important act of self-care is caring for your thoughts."

Have you heard of the equation E + R = O? It's not mathematical, or even scientific for that matter. It's a formula for success put forth by *The Success Principles* author and transformational speaker Jack Canfield. To break it down: E stands for Events, the circumstances and situations that appear in your life that you need to face and deal with; R is your Response to that event, how you handle it; and O is the Outcome based on how you responded to the event. Basically, Canfield is saying that every experience you have is the result of how you respond to what happens around you. The main concept is that each of us is completely responsible for our own responses, which ultimately creates our reality. We get to choose how we create our story. How do we make our decisions? Yes, with the thoughts that we think.

"You will attract into your life what you are, what requires healing, and what you consciously and subconsciously believe about yourself."

— Christine Gail

Whatever your starting point, you are fully responsible for making something of your life. Some people grow up with more advantages because they come from a wealthy family, had access to the finest teachers and schools, and had rich cultural experiences, while many people grew up poor and struggling, like me. However, we each have the power to change our circumstances by the way we respond to our surroundings. If you grew up with the thought that you were limited financially, you can now choose to believe it's an abundant world and the only thing holding you back from a truly abundant life is your thoughts.

If you lose your job, do you wallow in "Why me?" or try to figure out your next step? What energy are you putting forward to serve yourself? Are you placing blame on others for what is happening, or are you accepting the *what is-ness* of the situation and taking action to move on? Make it a point to release self-limiting beliefs and re-place them with new, empowering ones. You may not even realize you're blocking yourself from getting what you want by the sheer nature of your thoughts, which is why it's important to pay atten-tion to what you're thinking. What happens when you don't become aware of the thoughts that aren't serving you and allow them to take hold of you? You guessed it. Those thoughts will get in the way of your peace, your emotional state, and your progress. You can easily get stuck in negative self-talk and remain ineffective and unhappy, or you can choose to manage your thoughts and make them work in your favor.

When it comes to making decisions, base them on wanting the best for yourself and the belief that you deserve every bit of it. Decisions based on self-doubt and fear will only keep you stagnant and in a constant state of self-defeat. When your inner critic appears in your head, acknowledge it and then choose a better thought to think about. Once you learn how to manage your thoughts, you'll see your life improve on so many levels. And you'll know how to respond to any insecurities that pop up.

Although I'm sure you wish you could control everything that happens to you, there are always challenging plot twists along the way. When this happens, the one thing you do have control over is your thoughts. Again, your thoughts create your emotions, and since you're human, you're going to have emotional responses to situations. It's natural and necessary to let yourself feel the emotions fully, but try not to linger in them. As many therapists will attest, "Ya gotta feel it to heal it." Just don't stay there. You see, nothing can drag you down unless you choose to allow it. There's no escaping the ebbs and flows of life; just like Forrest Gump told the woman on a park bench, "Life is like a box of chocolates. You never know what you're gonna get." It's your job to take full responsibility for how you react and deal with the circumstances before you. You get to choose how you feel just by changing your thoughts.

What do you think? Are you ready to start being more conscious and choose more empowering thoughts?

WORDS MATTER

> *"Stop listening to your mind and start talking to your mind. Transform your inner critic to your inner coach."*
>
> — *Jack Canfield*

Now that you're armed with the information that you, and only you, control your thoughts and you can change them at any moment, you need to consider the words you speak and the actions you take. After all, your thoughts are expressed through words that, in turn, affect your emotions and subsequent actions. For now, let's concentrate on how you speak to yourself. Your subconscious has no filter and believes everything you say, so be careful about speaking negatively about yourself. The last thing you want to do is talk to yourself in a condescending and self-effacing way. Plenty of opinionated people can do that for you. Instead, what you need to do is be your own best friend and be kind, gentle, and loving to yourself. Be mindful of your thoughts and notice your inner dialogue. When you hear that inner voice of self-doubt, replace it with a thought that will bolster you. Consciously choose to change the phrase *I can't do this* to *I've got this!* Love yourself fully in thought, deed, and words because you're worth it. In other words (pun intended), be your own cheerleader and affirm how strong and capable you are.

One tool for boosting your self-esteem, motivating yourself, and replacing subconscious patterns is *Affirmations*. Simply put, affirmations are statements you create about yourself that retrain negative thoughts that no longer serve you while building your self-confidence.

Émile Coué, a late nineteenth century French psychologist and pharmacist, was the first to document use of affirmations for self-reprogramming. Although Coué believed in prescribing medications, he also believed in the power of autosuggestion. While treating his patients, he had them say to themselves out loud, many times throughout the day, *"Every day in every way, I am getting better and better.*" He noticed that these patients were curing themselves more effectively by replacing their *thought of illness* with a new *thought of cure*. He's now considered the father of modern-day affirmations for his groundbreaking use of a combination of drugs and autosuggestion.

Fast forward to the 1920s when a metaphysical writer named Florence Scovell Shinn brought New Thought spiritual teachings into the world. With her book *The Game of Life and How to Play It*, Shinn became the next pioneer in professing the benefits and power of affirmations. Shinn was also the mentor of Louise Hay. Hay taught that the words you think and speak control your success and happiness—she was the teacher who introduced me to the practice of affirmations.

One of my favorite Hay affirmations, which I use regularly, especially when I'm stressed, is, "*All is well in my world. Everything is working out for my highest good.*" When you believe everything is happening the way it's supposed to and perfectly timed, you allow peace to be your driving force.

Today, Erin Stutland is an "affirmations advocate." Stutland is a young, energetic teacher who created the program *Mantras in Motion*. With her background as a professional dancer, she combines affirmations with movement to intensify how you assimilate your words into your body. Every morning, I use one of her quick affirmation/body movements to "*step into the flow of life.*" I discovered Stutland during the coronavirus pandemic via a podcast on the Hay House radio broadcast, and I immediately took her online course. She even guides you through empowering walks outdoors by combining affirmations with exercise. If you'd like to check into her teachings, her website address is www.erinstutland.com.

To dive even deeper into how to incorporate affirmations more fully into your life, I suggest Betsy Finkelhoo's *Power Affirmation Journal*. It can be a useful addition to your journaling practice because it uses affirmations as a way to self-reflect, uplift your mind, and lead you to self-love and self-compassion. Finkelhoo also offers audio affirmations and affirmation empowerment group programs. You can find her affirmation meditations on the Insight Timer app and more information about her at www.finkelhoo.com.

Now that you know how effective and empowering affirmations can be, let's put them into practice. Affirmations usually start with the words "I am" and are positive and self-affirming. Let's try a few out for size. I'd like you to recite these statements out loud. Even if you don't believe what you're saying, say them anyway. Remember, the more you repeat your affirmations, the more you retrain your subconscious.

Repeat after me....

I am strong!
I am beautiful!
I am healthy!
I am confident!
I am peaceful!
I am enough!
I am worthy!
I am lovable!

I matter and my life matters!

I have what it takes to achieve my dreams!

Well done! Did you notice the exclamation mark after each statement? I did that intentionally because it's important for you to feel what you're saying. You have to say it like you mean it. When you create and use affirmations, be sure to tailor them to the areas where you feel you're lacking in something so you can reverse your story in that area. For instance, if you're doubting yourself, say, "I am fully capable of doing this." Or if you're feeling anxious, your affirmation would be, "I am peaceful and calm." In time, you'll automatically know and accept all your affirmations as the truth.

Affirmations are similar to the placebo effect, in which your thoughts communicate with your subconscious. A placebo effect is defined in the dictionary as, *a beneficial effect produced by a placebo drug or treatment, which cannot be attributed to the properties of the placebo itself, and must therefore be due to the patient's belief in that treatment.* Numerous scientific studies have been done on the validity of the placebo effect, which proves the power of self-talk, so use affirmations to your advantage.

And speaking of power....

YOUR BODY LANGUAGE MATTERS

Along with changing your thoughts, stories, and words, there's one last method of quickly altering your state of mind that can instantly make you feel empowered. That one thing is changing the way you physically move through your day.

Let's try something fun. Preferably standing in front of a mirror, I'd like you to pretend you are your favorite superhero. Visualize putting on your superhero cape and notice your posture. Is your head down? Are your shoulders pressed forward with your arms hanging down to your side in a defeated posture? I doubt it. Superheroes stand upright with their shoulders back, heads up, and their hands usually on their hips because they are powerful and strut their stuff. They own their superpowers and walk confidently through the world with that knowledge. You, too, were born with your own set of superpowers. Once you get to know yourself better and figure out your mission in this lifetime, you can visualize putting on your imaginary superhero cape at all times. Until you feel fully confident in who you are and what you have to offer, simply put on your cape and hold your head high. This simple gesture of changing your body language can translate to feeling and appearing more confident. It's the old saying, "Fake it till you make it!"

For a very long time, I relied on my imaginary superwoman cape and masked my way through the world. I really didn't know who I was, but I did my best to believe I did. People know me as upbeat, perky, energetic, and bubbly. Like the opening theme to *The Mary Tyler Moore Show*, I was the girl who could turn the world on with her smile. I've made a career performing on stages as a singer and dancer and continually share my talents, making others smile too. But what most people don't know is that beneath the surface, for a very long time, lurked a very damaged inner child.

Although I was born with a positive personality, my smile was often and unknowingly a survival mechanism to hide my sorrow and depression. It made me feel better to physically express happiness, even though I was broken inside. It was my quick fix and got me through my days. I had so much to learn about myself and the world, but at least I had control over that one simple technique of changing my physiology. As I came to recognize the lessons I'm sharing, my ear-to-ear smile became genuine because it was derived from pure joy. It's now real, authentic, and comes directly from the light within. I'm living with a sense of inner peace and have come full circle in wholeness back to the concepts of my hippie generation roots.

It's such a simple thing to do. Let's try it right now. Set a timer for thirty seconds and show your pearly whites—smile for thirty seconds. That's it! Hold it there for the full thirty seconds and see what happens. It may seem awkward at first, but the more you smile, the more you produce endorphins (the *feel-good* hormones). Studies suggest a direct correlation exists between smiling and our health. One study suggests smiling can even reduce stress.

Speaking of smiling, people often ask me why I'm so happy. The answer is I choose to dwell in positive energy instead of focusing on the doom and gloom in the world. (And there's plenty of it.) For my light to brighten up the lives of others, I have to keep shining. One way to do that is by recognizing all of the good around you and in all situations. Some people have called me a Pollyanna, to which I reply, "Maybe so, but Pollyanna lived a very happy life." (I borrowed that quote from channeler, Esther Hicks.) Even Ted Danson, the actor, said, "I am a bit of a Pollyanna. I spend most of my day happy." With our thoughts, we get to choose the vibes we wish to receive and send out, so doesn't it make sense to put joy and happiness at the top of the list?

HAVE AN ATTITUDE OF GRATITUDE

"Gratitude is the foundation for all abundance."

— *Eckhart Tolle*

A great way to reframe your thoughts is to focus on gratitude. Gratitude is one of the most powerful feelings you can generate to keep the flow of all good things coming your way. When you appreciate everything and everyone, you begin to see all of the good you already have. Your subconscious takes in all the positive aspects of your life and is retrained to look at the world in a positive light. When you focus your thoughts on the aspects that are working to your benefit, you'll get more of the same. Once you start viewing the beauty of your life with positivity and thankfulness, you'll begin seeing changes in yourself and your outlook. Richelle E. Goodrich, author of *Smile Anyway*, creatively said, "Gratitude paints little smiley faces on everything it touches."

Begin by noticing the magnificence of your body. It naturally knows what to do without any prompting from you. Your heart pumps blood on its own; your digestive system processes your food; you don't have to put any effort into breathing or walking or any other bodily functions that happen of their own accord. Our bodies are miraculous, and we take them for granted, yet they are what keep us functioning throughout our days. Be grateful for that.

Now, take a look at the abundance of love in your life. Do you have family and friends who support you, adore you, are there for you no matter what, and who want the very best for you? What a treasure trove you have if that's the case! When you walk through life appreciating the people who mean something to you, your heart becomes full and you can't help but feel blessed.

Let's move on to your surroundings. Look around you for a moment. Are you sitting in a comfortable chair or couch while reading this book? Do you have a roof over your head and running water? Do you own a car? Yes, these are very basic questions, but there are countries where running water, furniture, vehicles, and solid houses are a luxury. Appreciate what you have and you'll have more to appreciate.

Focusing your attention on everything good in your life will give you back more of the good stuff. Start paying attention to what makes you happy rather than your worries and concerns. You'll feel better and, in the process, you'll reprogram your brain to view the world through a different lens.

MINDFULNESS MATTERS

What comes to mind when you think about the word *mindfulness*? According to the Oxford Dictionary, it is defined as "a mental state achieved by focusing one's awareness on the present moment, while calmly acknowledging and accepting one's feelings, thoughts, and bodily sensations." And the Webster Dictionary says it's "the practice of maintaining a non-judgmental state of heightened or complete awareness of one's thoughts, emotions, or experiences on a moment-to-moment basis." Basically, it's a state of awareness, and all it asks of you is to pay attention to what's happening in you and around you. Mindfulness matters in all aspects of life, from the thoughts you think and the stories you tell yourself to the words you speak and the choices you make. What you focus on becomes your reality, so remain mindful of staying aligned with your vision of your ideal life.

> *"Realize deeply that the present moment is all you have. Make the now the primary focus of your life."*
>
> — *Eckhart Tolle*

As humans with busy lives, it's really easy to get stuck in our thoughts about our goals, our past regrets, and our ever-growing to-do list. While we spend time thinking about what could be and what we could have done better, we miss out on the fullness of our lives by dismissing the beauty of the present moment. Dwelling on a past that we wish had a different outcome is a natural tendency. But we can't change any of our history, so there's no use dwelling on it.

And although it's a great idea to have goals and prepare for the future, we don't need to live in that space either. We can visit our past and future, but our life is meant to be lived fully, one moment at a time, in the *now*. The past is done. Learn from it, grow, and keep moving full steam ahead. There's no need to beat yourself up over things that didn't work out. You did what you could with what you knew at the time.

And worrying about your future only causes unnecessary stress. You're creating stories that haven't even happened, and most of these false stories probably never will. Stay in the here and now because it's the only thing that's real.

Eckhart Tolle said, "Nothing has happened in the past; it happened in the Now. Nothing will ever happen in the future; it will happen in the Now." When you catch yourself stuck in non-productive thoughts about your past or unsettling thoughts about your future, stay mindful of living in the present moment. In the process of staying present, you can't help but soak up the richness of your existence. ***Let your presence in the present be a present to others.***

It's equally important to stay mindful of any negative thoughts that pop up that you find unsettling. If something doesn't feel right to you, it's a sign that you need to change your thoughts. Even when it comes to watching the news and witnessing devastation, riots, unrest, and violence, try your darnedest not to get swept into the vacuum. If you watch the news non-stop, you're going to carry that heaviness with you all the time. Author and Buddhist practitioner Jack Kornfield said, "A boulder is only heavy if you pick it up." The news can easily induce the lower energies of fear, sadness, frustration, anxiety, and anger, so my advice is to watch the news to learn what's going on in the world, and then let it go unless you feel a calling to do something productive to help solve the issues. Keep in mind that you'll be weighed down in proportion to the information you take in and carry with you throughout your day.

Byron Katie's book *Loving What Is* challenges you to question your thought patterns and get to the truth behind any negative or troubling thoughts and beliefs you may have. She provides you with four simple questions that will bring you to some very interesting conclusions once you go through the process. I used this technique when I was having a difficult time in a relationship, and it was eye-opening. The questions are: (1) Is it true? (2) Can I absolutely know it is true? (3) How do I react when I think that thought? (4) Who would I be without the thought? The final step is to turn the thought around by taking everything you said and reversing it. When you change the wording this way, you'll see that you might have been projecting or taking on a false belief. It's quite possible you might come away with an entirely different perspective on the situation. Not to be repetitive, but you get to choose your perspectives and your beliefs by the thoughts you think.

IT'S YOUR CHOICE

Everything in life is a choice—you get to choose, so be mindful of what choices you're making. Are they serving you or not? Are you causing yourself more stress by worrying about a future that hasn't happened yet? Are you staying in the present moment where everything is taking place in the here and now? Are you willing to let go of your past so you can embrace your future? Are you willing to accept that everything that happened to you in the past shaped you into who you are today? That past includes the relationships that didn't work out and the jobs that didn't feel right to you.

You *can* say yes or no to any thought. If you don't acknowledge and reframe the negative ones, you'll stay stuck and remain exactly where you are, and that may mean either being unhappy or settling for less than you could become. You get to choose how to write your own story.

Every day, with your thoughts, words, and actions, you're creating your reality. Choose peace; choose thoughts that feel better; choose to pursue your passions with gusto, fearlessness, and tenacity. Most of all, choose to believe in yourself. Tap into your inner world and connect with your ultimate power source. It's always there for the taking. And remember, there is no right or wrong path. Life will present you with the circumstances and opportunities you need to grow and learn. If the first path you take is unfulfilling and joyless, simply choose again.

To get there faster, be mindful of choosing and walking the pathways you intuitively know are right for you. When you choose to remain aligned with your spiritual connection, life seems to flow. Unexpected opportunities come your way and possibilities become endless. You can peacefully ride the waves rather than struggling to swim upstream. If you're open to good feeling thoughts, staying positive, and expecting everything will work out, you allow all of the goodness to come your way. It's all your choice! William Shakespeare said, "Nothing is, unless our thinking makes it so." So, whenever you catch yourself thinking fearful thoughts or having moments of insecurity or self-doubt, acknowledge them, let them go, change your story by reciting an affirmation that turns around your concerns, and *voilà*, you've just taken a huge step forward into your desired state of peace.

Here are a few exercises to help you start paying attention to your life. Ready? Here we go....

EXERCISE 1: AFFIRMATIONS

It's time to take out your trusty journal. Start your very own list of affirmations based on the areas of your life that you feel need to be strengthened. If you're struggling to feel good about yourself, this will lift you up. Even if you're skeptical about this working, try it because it's a way to keep feeding your subconscious positive, strong, healing thoughts about how amazing you are. Since you're reading this book, I encourage you to add the following affirmations each day—and say them like you mean it!

I am worthy!

I am good enough!

I matter!

I am confident!

I deserve to have my best life!

EXERCISE 2: CREATE A GRATITUDE JOURNAL

Part 1: The more you express gratitude, the more you'll have to be grateful about. This exercise will keep you tuned into an attitude of gratitude daily. Create a new Word document or get a new notebook and label it, "My Gratitude Journal." Start by putting today's date on it and making a list of everything and everyone you're grateful for. Every day, make a list of five things you're grateful for. It could be that someone let you go in front of them at the grocery store when you were in a hurry, or you had time for yourself to get a workout in, or you received an unexpected gift in the mail. There's always something, if not a lot of things, to appreciate every day. Many times, it's the simple things like a smile from someone when you were in a bad mood or how much you mellowed out by taking a walk or playing with your pet. It's best to write your list either first thing in the morning or as the last thing you do at night. That way you feed your subconscious positive, happy thoughts and attract more of the same.

Part 2: Some time during the day, just say *thank you* out loud to remind yourself that you have much to be thankful for.

EXERCISE 3: STAY MINDFUL OF YOUR MINDSET

Today, if anything comes up that makes you feel uncomfortable, stressed, or uneasy, take a moment to acknowledge the thought and then turn it around to a better thought. Remember, a thought can always be changed, and if a thought feels peaceful to you, stick with it. If something is worth writing about, open up that spanking new journal of yours! Get it out of your system and remember life is happening *for* you and not *to* you. This would be a great time to say your most empowering affirmations. Repeat after me....

I am strong!
I am peaceful!
I know everything is working out for my own good!
All is well in my world!

And if you're *really* stressed out, take a few minutes to close your eyes, take a few deep breaths, and clear your mind in the stillness. Turn all of your concerns over to the power that breathes you. It works. Try it.

Now that you're becoming more mindful of your thoughts, let's learn how to make them more effective. In the next chapter, you'll find more tools and techniques to assist you on your journey of happiness, fulfillment, and success. We're going to delve into practical tools to help you develop self-confidence and habits that will help you become more productive.

CHAPTER 5

YOU'VE GOT THIS!

"A man cannot be confident without his own approval."

— Mark Twain

Hold your head high. So far, you've defined what you want to have, be, and do in this lifetime, you've become more mindful of choosing self-serving thoughts, and you're tapping into your spiritual space, or considering doing so, to fully embrace all of who you are. It's now time to start believing in your abilities and develop self-confidence. In this chapter, you'll find tools to help you do just that.

When you're in show business, you have to be prepared to face your worst critics. I learned this early on in my career when I landed the lead role of Luisa in *The Fantasticks* at a local dinner theater. Although it wasn't my first lead role, since I had already portrayed Dorothy in *The Wizard of Oz* and I had a few other lead roles in high school, I was still very inexperienced and just beginning to discover the nuances of my singing voice. I was certainly no match to the lyrical soprano range this role required, but I was young and must have looked the part. As much as I did my best, I received a nasty review from a local reporter who said my voice "literally ruined every number I sang." It was harsh, and I took it really hard. Those words kept repeating over and over in my head. It was difficult to get past them because I allowed them to stew within my memory bank, which would bring me down. What it didn't do, however, was stop my desire to keep singing and dancing. I kept performing, and the more I was on stage, the stronger my confidence became.

Although it's true that we all love being acknowledged and applauded for our talents, and that the more accolades we receive, the more confident we become, it's important to know that true confidence comes from within. You have to believe in yourself and your capabilities. Staying connected to your inner world and developing new habits are your best bet for remaining aligned with yourself and keeping yourself centered and focused on becoming your best self.

As the old adage goes, to get something you never had, you have to do something you never did. As you go through your days, you create routines along the way that either work in your favor or do the exact opposite and hold you back. If you've always wanted to be in great shape but continually overeat and don't exercise enough, you're never going to get that fit body you're dreaming about. You need to develop new habits that work for you and not against you. Confidence develops when you connect all the facets of your mind, body, and spirit. As Neale Donald Walsch, author of *Conversations with God*, said, "The body and mind are tools for the agenda of the soul." On that note, here are some productivity techniques and practices I've incorporated into my daily routine that I feel can help you develop confidence and self-esteem. There's always more to learn, more room to grow, and more ways to keep us centered, happy, and peaceful while we pursue our dreams. Find the practices that feel right for you.

GET YOUR DAILY DOSE OF M&MS!

No, I don't mean the plain or peanut type. I'm talking about incorporating the following daily habits: Morning Rituals, Meditation, Mindfulness, Movement, and Music. Each of these components will facilitate your quest to become more self-aware and centered, which will lead you to becoming more courageous and fearless. We already discussed the topic of mindfulness in the last chapter, so now we're going to talk about what you do when you first wake up.

One of the most powerful ways to fast-track your life and help you walk self-assuredly in the world is to start off your day with empowering morning routines. By taking one, some, or all of the suggestions in this chapter, you'll not only become fearless, but you'll have days that are more productive. Harvard researchers have found that the first hour of your day dictates how the rest of your day will go. If you ask extremely successful people about their habits, they say their morning routine is essential to their productivity. A morning routine means setting aside segments of time to sit silently, journal, recite affirmations, exercise, work on self-development in some fashion, and do the one pressing priority item that absolutely needs to get done before you start off your day.

MORNINGS MATTER

Anyone who knows me personally knows I'm *not* a morning person and usually eat breakfast around 2 p.m., so when I speak of mornings, I'm talking about whatever time you wake up to greet the day and are feeling well rested. It's a known fact that the most successful people are early risers, so I encourage you to do that if you can. I've tried many times to switch over to a morning schedule, but my body has always been programmed to wake up late. Countless mornings when I was growing up, I'd hear my mother shouting, "Gloria Lynn, get out of bed!" (That was the only time she used my middle name.) If you're a morning person, great. If you're like me, do your best to get up a tiny bit earlier to start your day in a positive and focused way.

What's the first thing you do when you wake up? Do you reach for your phone to check your messages, texts, email, and voicemail? Do you grab a cup of coffee and start working on your to-do list? Do you take care of others before taking care of yourself? If any of this sounds familiar, there's a better way.

Many people go about their days on automatic pilot, disregarding their inner world. They end up stressed out, anxious, and overwhelmed. If your desire is to have a gratifying, enjoyable, and fulfilling day, it's best to incorporate positive morning habits into your daily routine. This will get you off on the right foot feeling more centered and grounded. It is a way to power-up your day, which will power-up your goals and dreams.

Let's start from the beginning of your morning. One tip I've learned is to keep your phone away from your bed so when your alarm goes off, you're forced to get out of bed and not just hit the snooze button. If you're always struggling to find more time in the day, you'll need to make the time, and this little trick will keep you from lingering in bed too long, which can waste your precious time. Once you're out of bed, make it a habit to turn your alarm off and not look at your phone right away. This keeps you from instantly bombarding your brain with to-do lists and stress instead of using the calm energy of your freshly awakened brain to start out the day with peace, clarity, and focus. Creating a practice in which you care for yourself first before allowing all of the busyness of your life to take hold of you is in your best interest.

Now that your eyes are open and you're in an upright position, do a few stretches to wake up your body. While you're stretching, welcome your day with a simple positive statement that makes you feel grateful to be alive. It could be something like, "It's a good day to have a good day!" or "Good morning, life!" If you've ever seen the movie *Pee Wee Herman's Big Adventure*, think of the scene where he jumps out of bed ready and excited to greet the day. He loves his life and soon you will too.

Personal development expert Mary Morrissey suggests another way to start your day on a positive note is to give a physical thumbs up to the Universe for giving you the day. I suggest giving two thumbs up, not only to being alive, but to the beautiful life you're creating, and two thumbs up to yourself because you know you're on your way to the life of your dreams.

It's important to clear your mind first thing in the morning. Some may choose to take a walk or do some type of physical exercise while others may write in their journals to work out any issues they're dealing with. I know a few people who talk to themselves to clear their heads. Whatever works for you to release your worries and concerns will do the trick, but make sure you do just that. You don't want to carry the weight of your emotional baggage on your shoulders all day. It's important to let go of your concerns, and even more powerful when you surrender them to your Higher Power, which is that ever-present energy in and around us that co-creates our days.

Those who like to journal find this first-thing-in-the-morning technique extremely beneficial. Try this routine for at least a week to see if it works for you. It's a four-step process and begins with a morning *dump*. Bathroom jokes aside, it's not that kind of dump, although it's similar. A *brain dump* is the process of releasing the toxicity stored in your brain. This clears your mind to start the day fresh. Julia Cameron, author of *The Artist's Way*, called her journaling technique the *Morning Pages*. In this method, you simply write three pages of stream of consciousness thoughts detailing what's on your mind. I use a modified version of this exercise (listed below) in which I include questions from motivational coach Erin Stutland. She combined the *dump* with a productivity tool called the *One Thing* where you write down the one priority item that absolutely needs to get done. This was based on the Pomodoro Method of time blocking written about in Gary Keller's book, *The ONE Thing: The Surprisingly Simple Truth Behind Extraordinary Results.*

Step 1: The *Morning Pages* Brain Dump

With or without your morning cup of coffee in hand, here are a few questions and activities to guide you along. Write whatever you're feeling, no-holds-barred. This is your time to get things out of your system.

1. What's going on in your inner world? What's bothering you?

2. What fears or beliefs are you buying into right now?

3. Create an affirmation based on the opposite of what you fear.

4. Ask the Universe for help.

5. Write down the *one* thing you want to do today to move your life forward.

When you've sufficiently dumped your cares, the next step is to tap into your spiritual center through meditation. You've already released your worries through the *Morning Pages*, so it's time to recharge and look inward to start your day in a peaceful, intentional way.

Step 2: Making Conscious Contact With Your Inner World

"Listen to the silence. It has so much to say."

— Rumi

I know, I know...who has time to sit still in our busy world? I've always been action-oriented. I thought my daily yoga stretches along with my ability to get into a zone doing what I loved and my calm, easygoing personality were enough to carry me through my days. But when my enormous task list and multiple projects felt overwhelming and stressed me out, I knew I had to find balance somehow or I would burn out and get physically sick. I needed to upgrade to a deeper state of calm.

Around this time, I received an email from the Mindvalley Community offering a course by a former Broadway performer named Emily Fletcher on a new type of meditation she called the "M-Word" (M for Meditation). It was marketed as *Modern Meditation* and a way of becoming more centered, focused, and productive. Since this came at a time when my to-do lists were becoming un-manageable, I figured I'd give it a shot. To my surprise, as each day progressed, I became more and more focused, centered, peaceful, and yes, productive. It worked. For this reason, I encourage you to try to incorporate meditation into your daily routine. If you'd like to try this particular technique, you can find more information on the Ziva Meditation website: www.zivameditation.com.

Meditation comes in many forms and may encompass breathing exercises, chanting, mantras (silently repeating a word or phrase once your mind starts to wander), setting an intention (doing so first thing in the morning works best), gratitude, and affirmations. If you're familiar with Wii gaming boards, you know when you turn one on, a little voice says, "Connecting, connecting, connecting." In a similar fashion, when you meditate, you're connecting to your spiritual center, which will guide you in the game of life. This is your time to hook up to your power source.

Although I highly recommend taking time to sit and be still in silence, there's no right or wrong way to meditate. It's simply the practice of quieting your mind and listening in the silence. It's a way to relax, reboot, and recharge your energies. Have you noticed you think a lot when you're in the shower? That's because you don't have the distractions of your cell phone, TV, or other people. It's just you and your thoughts. Your Higher Self talks to you quite a bit when you're alone. Many people get their most creative ideas when they relax in stillness. Anything that takes you out of your busy state and into one of peace is a form of meditation. You can do this by taking a walk in nature, doing yoga, cooking, or even driving (but keep your eyes on the road!). I love doing dishes and laundry for this very reason. It's my alone time. We all need such time daily to keep ourselves balanced.

To get the full benefit of meditation, however, I've found the best way to connect with your inner world deeply is to close your eyes and release the inner chatter and concerns of the day. Unlike the advice in the last chapter about consciously changing your thoughts to change your story, this is a process of letting go. You are so much more than your thoughts. You are the observer of your thoughts, and the practice of meditation is simply being a witness to them. It's not the time to reflect upon, judge, or analyze what comes into your awareness, but rather a time to let go of any attachment to it. It's your time to let go of the past and future and free yourself to be in the present moment. It's also the time to become familiar with your inner space.

Most meditations start with breathing exercises because breathing calms your body. It's a physical method of connecting the mind, body, and spirit. Your breath is your life force and automatically keeps you alive. We don't normally pay attention to it unless we're stressed out, panicked, or in the middle of exercising and become conscious that we're breathing heavily. The act of mindful breathing has been shown to lower your heart rate, decrease stress, calm your nerves, and bring you into the present moment. And for the purpose of achieving your dreams, it will help you perform better throughout the day with a clearer focus on your tasks.

Here are a few breathing exercises to get you going.

The first technique, as taught by Emily Fletcher of the M-Word method, is called the Balancing Breath. It is the one I use most often. A nerve fiber membrane in the middle of your brain, called the corpus callosum, links the right and left hemispheres. This particular breathing exercise brings oxygen to that membrane and increases its thickness, which strengthens that connection. The right side is where your creativity, ideas, and intuition reside, whereas the left side is your logical, analytical, and critical side. Many people spend too much time operating from their left brain. This breathing exercise will help balance that out so fresh ideas, insights, and creativity will emerge. It's called alternate nostril breathing. Here's how to do it:

1. Take your right thumb and close your right nostril.

2. Take a deep inhale through your left nostril.

3. Release your right thumb, and close the left nostril with your ring finger.

4. Exhale through your right nostril.

5. Inhale through your right nostril.

6. Go back to step one, and repeat the above steps several times.

The second technique involves counting and is a three-step process of inhaling, holding the breath, and then exhaling, but you breathe in various rhythms. The most common is the 4-4-4 method, also known as *Box Breathing*.

Try this:

1. Deeply inhale through your nose to a count of four. Start the inhale from your belly and let the air rise through your chest. Fill your lungs completely. Your abdomen should feel like a filled-up balloon.

2. Hold the breath for a count of four.

3. Exhale slowly for a four count through either your nose, mouth, or pursed lips (like you're blowing through a straw). Experiment with the exhale to see if releasing through your nose or mouth makes you feel more relaxed.

4. Repeat these three steps until you feel calm.

Once you get the hang of that, try different rhythms. For instance, you can do combinations of 4-4-8 where you inhale to a count of four, hold for four, and exhale for an eight count, or 4-7-8 where you hold for a seven count.

To go even deeper with the rhythmical breathing exercises, add a few silent phrases upon inhalation and exhalation. For instance, when you breathe in, silently say, "peace" and on the exhale, silently say, "I let go" to release concerns, fears, or toxicity. Breathe in peace, and breathe out your worries.

As a side note, at any point in your day when you feel overwhelmed, anxious, or totally stressed out, give yourself a mindful moment simply to close your eyes and breathe. Pay attention to your inhalation and exhalation, and try out one of the breathing techniques outlined above. If you prefer technology, there are apps for that, which guide you through rhythmical breathing. I like the *Calm* app because it allows you to set the duration and gives you a visual so you can look down at the phone with your eyes half shut and follow the visual. This is a free app unless you get the premium service (as is the case with most apps). Similarly, if you have an Apple watch, set it to the breathe mode and inhale and exhale to its visuals and/ or haptics, where you feel a gentle pulse on your wrist for the inhalation. You can also simply set the timer on your phone for five minutes and just breathe until you feel a sense of calm come over you. Do whichever works best for you. The goal is to use this as a shortcut to relax, reboot, and recharge.

One of the most thorough programs pertaining to managing our breath is from Stig Severinsen, who holds the Guinness world record for holding his breath underwater—a whopping twenty-two minutes! He's mastered the art of breath control and knows the advantages of mindful breathing include building a powerful immune system, reducing inflammation, getting a better night's sleep, healing your body, and a host of other benefits. If you're interested in finding out more about his program, check out his book, *Breatheology: The Art of Conscious Breathing*, or go to his website, www.breathology.com, where he offers online courses.

Let's talk about the science of meditation's effects on the body. The combination of meditation and mindfulness serves to strengthen the connections in the nervous system. Every time you take a deep breath, you're activating the vagus nerve, which is the longest cranial nerve and passes through the neck and thorax to the abdomen. It's one of the main connectors from your brain to your body and is responsible for regulating your internal organs, heart rate, and respiration. By stimulating this nerve, you send a message to your body that it's time to relax, which leads to long-term improvements in your mood and wellbeing.

According to a healthline.com article by Matthew Thorpe and Rachael Link, there are twelve science-based benefits of meditation:

Meditation can reduce stress, control anxiety, promote emotional health, enhance self-awareness, lengthen attention span, improve sleep, help control pain, decrease blood pressure, reduce age-related memory loss, generate kindness, and help fight addictions.

Additionally, in an interview with the *Washington Post*, Harvard neuroscientist Sara Lazar supplied an overview of how meditation affects the brain. Since science isn't my thing, I'll just briefly recap the areas of the brain she addressed and leave it up to you to delve deeper into these aspects.

The first area Lazar says is affected is the left hippocampus, which is the part of the brain that helps us learn and where our cognitive ability and memory reside. Research confirms that meditation causes the hippocampus to grow in volume and thickness and for gray-matter density to increase, which enhances its function.

The second area of the brain affected by meditation is the posterior cingulate, which relates to wandering thoughts and self-relevance. The more we meditate, the larger and stronger the posterior cingulate gets, which makes it easier to focus, stay in the present moment, and observe without judgment.

The third region meditation strengthens is called the pons (originating from the Latin word for *bridge*). The pons is located in the middle of the brain stem. It is involved in many of our essential functions, including sleep, facial expressions, processing sensory input, and basic physical function.

The fourth area is the temper parental junction (TPF), which is associated with empathy and compassion.

And the fifth section of the brain affected is the amygdala, known as the area from which our *fight or flight* reactions emanate. Unlike the other sections of the brain that grow with meditation, the amygdala shrinks, which makes us less likely to get caught up in fear-based responses.

Another study recently posted by the *International Journal of Arts, Humanities & Social Sciences* involved people with intellectual and developmental disabilities. It concluded that, "Mindfulness meditation-based practices can lead to positive outcomes such as reductions in aggression, increased social functioning and interactions with peers, and feelings of calmness."

Yes, meditation is a mighty powerful and helpful tool, so my advice is at least to give it a whirl and see if it makes a difference.

Along with the many ways to meditate, there are equally as many teachers to guide you along. If you have a smartphone, you can find tons of guided meditations on the App Store. Are you ready to amplify your life and dive inward? If so, here are a few meditation apps I personally use and recommend.

- Insight Timer—This contains 100,000 guided audio meditations, and it's free. You can set the duration of your meditation and any topic you feel you need to address at the moment. It also offers more than 700 courses, which are in-app purchases that may be appealing to you.

- Unplug—Although it isn't free, Unplug delivers content through video, so you get to see the instructor as if you're in a class. It's professionally done and covers every topic you could possibly need. You get a seven-day free trial, and if you wish to continue, you are charged a minimal monthly or yearly fee. I suggest checking it out if only for the seven-day trial to get inspired. Check out the morning meditation called *Today Is Going to Be A Great Day* by Suze Yalof Schwartz. It will start you off on the right foot with great questions to ask yourself during your meditation, like, "What could go right today?" and "What will be your favorite part of this day?"

- Hay House Unlimited Audio—For a minimal monthly subscription fee, which is worth it, you are offered more than 30,000 hours of audiobooks, podcasts, radio shows, and interviews along with the meditations.

If you prefer to grab things off of the internet, go to YouTube and type in the phrase *guided meditations.* Voilà! You'll find thousands of free meditations at your fingertips. Just like the Insight Timer app, you can search according to your specific needs and/or how much time you have to spend meditating. For instance, if you only have five minutes to spare in the morning, type in *five-minute guided morning meditation* or *meditations for stress and anxiety* or *meditations for a restful night's sleep.* Whatever your soul needs, meditation is the answer.

Some of my favorite meditation teachers are Deepak Chopra, David Ji, Sarah Blondin, Emily Fletcher, Jack Canfield, and Eckhart Tolle. I know you'll find your own favorites from the many options as soon as you fall into your own habitual meditation groove. You'll come out of it feeling lighter, invigorated, peaceful, and appreciative of all the goodness in your life. The more you do it, the more you'll see things start to change within and how life seems to flow more easily. You'll find that your serenity is in the silence.

*"We dance round in a ring and suppose,
but the Secret sits in the middle and knows."*

— Robert Frost

One way I enter the stillness is by using the phrase, "Be still, and know that I am God" (Psalm 46:10). As you know, I'm not religious, but this Bible verse speaks to me because I believe God lives in us, through us, and is all around us. We are all divine sparks of that powerful energy source.

1. Find a comfortable chair and sit upright with your palms facing upwards in your lap. Start by closing your eyes. Take a few deep breaths in and out through your nose. Do this a few more times. If anything is on your mind, set it free. Let go of any worries or concerns and feel the release. Just be still and breathe. Now bring this phrase silently to your attention in your mind. "Be still, and know that I am God." We're going to slowly start chopping off the ends of this phrase as follows:

2. Silently say the phrase, "Be still, and know that I am God." Whatever your concept of God is, know that you are connected to it at this very moment just by noticing its presence. Sit with it, and feel its energy moving through each cell of your body.

3. Now silently say, "Be still, and know that I am." Ask yourself, "Who am I? What is my true spiritual nature?" Don't overthink it; just let the answers pop into your head.

4. Moving on… "Be still, and know." Know that you are a divine being of light and love and that all is well in your world. Life always works out for your own good.

5. "Be still." There's nothing for you to do but be here, right now, in this moment. Feel your sense of openness and vastness.

6.   Our last silent mantra…is "Be." Just be you as you are now, connected to your Higher energies, and honor the light inside you. Your true self is a radiant being of light. You're free. You're limitless. You're powerful. You're meant to be here…right here, right now.

You can open your eyes when you feel sufficiently recharged.

(Please note: As a reader of this book, you can get a free recorded version of this meditation by visiting my website: www.PowerUpYourDreams.com.)

Once you add the *Morning Pages* and meditation to your daily routine, you'll see a shift in how you feel throughout the day. When issues and challenges arise, you'll be more equipped to deal with them calmly and peacefully. You'll have a clearer head and have more productive days. This has been my experience, as it has been for millions of people around the world. It makes sense to give it a shot. And if it works for you, try to add it to your daily morning mix.

No magic number exists for how long it takes to form a habit, but studies have shown it takes anywhere from two months to one year to create and reinforce new habits. In 2009, Phillippa Lally and her colleagues at the University College London published a study in the *European Journal of Social Psychology* that found it took an average of sixty-six days to form a habit. Commit to going *all-in* and make a promise to yourself to change your disempowering habits into new empowering ones. Commitment is key to making lasting changes, so do the things that serve you. Once the new habits become automatic, you'll begin seeing changes.

Along with working with your inner world, it's ultra-important to take action steps to push you along. Without taking a step each day toward your goals, you're going to remain in the same spot. That's not what you want to do when you have a burning desire in your heart to be somewhere else. Remember the five actions associated with the *brain dump*? The last was, "*Write down the* one *thing you want to do today to move your life forward.*" This is not only a thought on a piece of paper; it's also an action step you must take.

It's best to take care of this item in the morning after you're done journaling and/or meditating, but ideally, you want to be at peak performance when you take this action. If you're tired when you wake up because you didn't get enough sleep, and you're not at your best at that time, take care of your one important task later in the day when you're feeling more alert and able to be fully present. That being said, I highly recommend you take care of your one important task first thing because, as you know, distractions occur throughout the day, and you're more prone to forget or neglect your action step. I've had to push myself many times to get the task done right off the bat. But I've learned that if I didn't get it done early, it didn't get done at all. Not taking these little strides forward was a form of self-sabotage. Not good.

Two other modifications of the morning routine are also equally ef-fective and include the M&Ms. The first method is called the *Hour of Power* as taught by Jack Canfield, author of *The Success Principles*. He suggests that you split up the first hour of the day into twenty minutes of exercise, twenty minutes of meditation, and twenty min-utes of reading something inspirational, motivational, or developmental. This regime taps into your mind, body, and spirit and sets you up to greet the world as your best self.

I also recommend Hal Elrod's routine called *The Miracle Morning*. He suggests very short segments of *habit stacking*, using six factors he combined into the acronym, SAVERS. These incorporate the aspects of Silence (in the form of meditation, prayer, or contemplation), Affirmations, Visualization (which we'll cover in Chapter 7), Exercise, Reading, and Scribing (writing/journaling). Each of these components can be done for five to ten minutes, or you can pick and choose the ones that work for you and make your own schedule. Elrod felt so strongly about the value of morning regimes that he made an entire documentary on it. You can find it on Amazon Prime or Vimeo on Demand under miraclemorning.com.

Whichever new practices you decide to adopt, remember that this is your power hour, and you'll be creating new habits to keep you on track while moving forward feeling inspired and motivated. Do you remember the old cartoon *Mighty Mouse*? In the opening, you see a very buff mouse flexing his muscles and then flying into the air accompanied by his anthem, "Here I come to save the day!" This is how I'd like you to attack your mornings. Know with utmost confidence that your new habits are going to save your day and fly you to new heights!

To recap, it's extremely beneficial to incorporate a morning routine that includes journaling, exercising, meditating, reading, and doing the one priority item you need to get done. Make your morning work for you and life will flow much more easily.

On that note, let's work on getting you set up with a morning power hour.

Step 1: Get some sleep.

It all starts the night before. Decide what time you'll go to sleep and what time you'll wake up. Most people require seven to eight hours of sleep to function at their best, so plan accordingly. Set a reminder to alert you when it's time to turn everything off and get to bed.

Step 2: Plan it.

Decide how many minutes you'd like to assign to journaling, exercising, reading, and doing your *one thing*. You don't need to do them all, but make sure you wake up your mind and body and tune into your spiritual center in some fashion.

Step 3: Do it.

Take action tomorrow morning. Try your new morning routine for at least thirty days—ideally, two months to make it stick. You'll tweak your routine as you go and find what works best for you. The important thing is to commit to yourself and your new way of starting your day. I highly recommend adding time to meditate in the morning to start your day off in the most productive and focused way.

In the next chapter, we're going to focus on the last M&Ms—movement and music—and how to best take care of your body. Let's *move* on then, shall we?

CHAPTER 6

DANCE TO THE MUSIC

"If you take care of your body, it'll take care of you."

— *Oprah Winfrey*

So far, we've talked about changing your thoughts and tuning into your inner world. Now we're going to focus on taking care of your exterior since, after all, we're having a human experience in human form. Your body is an amazing machine that works perfectly if you know how to take care of it. It's your vehicle to get you through this lifetime and needs regular maintenance to keep it healthy and working in tip-top condition.

When I was sixteen, I stopped dancing to start working. My once tight, firm body slowly began turning into a flabby, pillow-like texture because of the lack of exercise and my habit of eating junk food to quell my inner pain and anxiety. With a five-foot, four-inch frame, the weight gain was obvious, and I couldn't look at myself in the mirror without feeling disgusted. My self-esteem and self-love were nowhere to be found. It was the lowest point of my youth.

During this time, I started binge eating and the roots of my emotional eating patterns began to form. I tried out different diets and was a bit bulimic, swallowing teaspoons of mustard to force myself to throw up. Everything was a temporary fix, which eventually backfired, and I went back to consuming too many Devil Dogs, Ring Dings, chips, and pints of ice cream.

I went from being a straight A student in grammar school to flunking out of classes in my junior year of high school. I was a complete mental and emotional mess and, as previously mentioned, I entertained thoughts of ending my life. I never mentioned this to anyone and just put on my pretend smile to get through the days. My only moments of joy were my involvement in the high school plays and music classes.

Things turned around senior year when I became friends with a few girls who accepted me for who I was. I joined the color guard. Marching with flags and twirling heavy fake guns was a fun addition to my theater productions. I became more social and began dancing in my living room while no one was watching. People started telling me I looked more in shape, and simultaneously, my grades went back up and my weight started dropping. Not only did I feel better about myself, but I was getting external validation that I looked better and seemed happier.

Over the years, I came to learn that the way you look doesn't matter, but how you *feel* about the way you look is important to your confidence. When you like what you see in the mirror, you walk with confidence through the world, but if you don't like what you see, it affects your ability to love yourself. Can you look at yourself in the mirror right now and tell yourself, "I love you"? Can you accept that you're perfect just the way you are and that you, just like the rest of us, are a work in progress? Instead of hating on the areas of your body that you don't like, learn how to change your shape, and increase your fitness.

We're all perfectly imperfect. Try to embrace that notion and let go of any negative self-talk when it comes up. FYI, I battle with self-criticism constantly, but I have the knowledge and tools to stop doing it by changing my thoughts and reciting affirmations. I no longer base my self-worth on what people think of me. I now know that taking care of myself is not just about physical exercise but also involves being mindful of my inner world. It goes hand in hand.

It's a no-brainer that the basics of taking care of your body include exercising, making healthy food choices, and drinking lots of water. As with everything, remain aware of the types of foods you consume and make it a habit to move your body.

The human body is made up of more than 60 percent water, so it's important to drink enough of it every day to flush out toxins, maintain a healthy weight, and keep your energy up. Drinking enough water is important to the functions of every organ, tissue, and cell in your body. According to WebMD, every day you should drink between half an ounce and an ounce of water for each pound you weigh. If you weigh 130 pounds, you want to drink sixty-five to 130 ounces of water a day. I usually carry bottles of water with me everywhere I go to ensure I'm getting enough.

When it comes to exercise, much like life in general, find things that make you feel alive and in-the-moment and you look forward to doing. Otherwise, you're going to get bored quickly and find excuses not to do them. Experiment with different types of physical activities if you're not sure what floats your boat. Take some classes you think you might like; go outside and walk, jog, or run; engage in some kind of sport; or pull up some exercise apps on your phone. (If I'm short on time, I use the apps FitOn, 7MWC [7 Minute Workout Challenge] and Workout for Women because they offer short and effective routines.) Whatever makes you feel exhilarated and activates your endorphins and dopamine *feel-good* levels is the ticket to consistency.

If you keep at it, you're going to enjoy the fruits of having the energy and vitality to carry out your purpose. For me, coming from a dance background and knowing how my body responds to different types of workouts, I found that weight training was one of the best ways to reshape my body. Aerobics will get your heart in shape, but if you want to see actual progress in the mirror, add weight training to your regime. For this reason, I took a liking to Jazzercise classes, which incorporate both dance moves and weight routines. It was fun, and I got to hang with like-minded women who were on a quest to stay in shape. When you find and follow exercise routines you enjoy, exercise will no longer be at the bottom of your to-do list.

Another great way to get energized is to put on your favorite music and dance! When I started dancing in my living room, it instantly made me feel lighter on the inside. In those moments, nothing else mattered. The music took me to a different headspace, and my body automatically became an expression of that liberating feeling. I didn't fully realize it then, but music and dancing were my true passions, and without them, I didn't feel complete.

Whatever makes you feel free, light, and joyful is what your soul wants you to continue doing. If dancing isn't your thing, I encourage you to use music to move into a different state of being. The goal is to experience a peaceful, easy, happy state of mind and lift yourself up. Sometimes, especially when we're stressed out, anxious, depressed, frustrated, sad, angry, or lost in our thoughts, just putting on music will ease the tension.

Let's take a look at how music changes your brain chemistry. For one, it helps you learn better, which is why you're taught the alphabet in song format. I had a wonderful music teacher in grammar school who created a song for the preamble of the Constitution, and to this day, I can still recite it. Isn't it funny how we can remember lyrics to songs we heard as kids but can't remember what we had for lunch yesterday?

Music is also a mood regulator. It releases the neurotransmitter dopamine, which makes you feel good. Certain songs relax you and others energize you. When you listen to sad music, it's soothing because your body creates the hormone prolactin, which is what mothers produce when they're breastfeeding babies. You can also produce the not-so-helpful stress hormone, cortisol, which can go up or down depending on whether or not you like the music.

Music can boost your immune system by increasing the number of natural killer cells in your system and increasing Immunoglobulin A, an antibody that plays a vital role in the immune function of mucus membranes. According to a 2014 study of the effects of music preference on functional brain connectivity, listening to a favorite song, no matter what type of music, enhances the connectivity between auditory brain areas and the hippocampus, a region responsible for memory and social emotion consolidation. This may explain the changes in our mental and emotional states.

Many different areas of the brain are affected by music, according to studies using MRI (magnetic resonance imaging) and PET (positron emission tomography) scans. Playing an instrument uses different areas of your brain than just listening. Mounting evidence suggests a positive correlation between music training and cognitive function, especially when the training starts at a young age.

In the article "Musicians Have More Connected Brains Than Non-Musicians," NeurosienceNews.com cited a study that found musicians had stronger functional connectivity (the synchronized activity of brain regions) in the auditory regions of both brain hemispheres. They also noted that musicians had stronger white matter connections between auditory regions and lobes involved in various types of high-level processing. Despite the article's title, I have no intention of casting judgment. I'm just presenting a few scientific facts. Everything we learn helps us grow.

Stick with your joy, but keep in mind that whenever you learn something new, you're building and using more brain space. For a more in-depth and interactive look at which parts of the brain are affected by listening to music, check out the article "Your Brain on Music" from the University of Florida, which you can find in the Resources section.

I'd like to give a huge shout out to Joe Scott of the *Answers with Joe* podcast regarding his "How Music Hacks the Brain" video. It guided me in the right direction in a very entertaining way.

Music is so powerful that it's used as therapy to treat people with emotional, cognitive, and physical issues. In 2013, the American Psychological Association posted an article titled "Music as Medicine," which recognized how music is an effective form of therapy for providing an emotional outlet. Researchers conducted studies on how song, sound frequencies, and rhythm can treat physical ailments in premature babies, people with depression, and people with Parkinson's. Years later, they were able to document improvement in all three scenarios.

From my own experience, I've done many gigs in nursing homes where physically debilitated seniors sat in the community room in their wheelchairs with their heads down, looking like they had been lobotomized, but once the music came on and I started singing, their heads popped up. I could see them come alive and awaken to the present moment. Something was triggered deep inside them, making their fingers snap, or they'd move their lips to sing along with me. It was amazing to witness how the magic of music brought them back to life, even if just for an hour.

Edward O. Wilson, author of *The Social Conquest of Earth*, said, "To create and perform music is a human instinct. It is one of the true universals of our species." No matter where you live on our beautiful planet, music can heal, soothe, and excite your soul!

Let's go back to our M&Ms for a moment. So far, we've talked about managing your mornings, meditating, mindfulness, movement, and music. Another M word has to do with what we put on our forks—our *meals*.

"Sorry. There's no magic bullet. You gotta eat healthy and live healthy to be healthy and look healthy. End of story."

— *Morgan Spurlock*

Just like we need to put clean gas in our cars for them to run efficiently, we need to fuel our bodies with whole foods rather than processed junk, which only serves to spike our sugar levels and can lead to all kinds of physical problems, which, in turn, lead to psychological problems. According to a Harvard Medical School blog on Nutritional Psychiatry, studies have compared traditional diets, like the Mediterranean diet and the traditional Japanese diet, to a typical Western diet and have shown that the risk of depression is 25 to 35 percent lower in those who eat a traditional diet. Scientists attribute this difference to these traditional diets focusing on vegetables, fruits, unprocessed grains, and fish/seafood, and containing only modest amounts of lean meats and dairy. They are also void of processed and refined foods and sugars, which are staples of the Western diet.

Taking care of your body involves being mindful of your food choices. Ensure you get a balance of proteins (lean meats, chicken, fish), complex carbohydrates (fruits, vegetables, and whole grains), and small amounts of good fats, like avocados, olives, and nuts. And if you're vegetarian, make sure you're getting enough protein. Of the many different diets out there, most share the theme of avoiding sugar and processed foods.

Ideally, a pristine mix of these healthy foods will keep your blood sugar levels stable and your energy up. Most likely, you'll find that your cravings for the less healthy foods will diminish. However, as you know, there will be times when you're either on vacation, at a party, out with friends at a restaurant, or at a holiday get-together where you're surrounded by foods that could be detrimental to your health. So what do you do when you have a choice either to eat your normal "clean" diet or indulge in your favorite high-calorie meal followed by a delectable dessert? I suggest you order what you want, dig in and enjoy every bite, but pay attention to the portion sizes. The key is not to eat mindlessly until you're stuffed, but to be mindful of how much you're eating.

I don't recommend dieting at all. It will only make you feel deprived of the things you enjoy. The main thing with any kind of weight-loss program is to become aware of what you're eating, why you're eating, how much you're eating, and your emotional state when you're eating. When you crave sugary sweets or salty snacks, are you just craving a more satisfying life and using food as a temporary fix?

Weight gain is something I've battled with since I was sixteen. When I learned that *stressed* spelled backward is *desserts*, I became a sugar junkie. Back in the '60s and '70s, there was very little information on how to eat well, so I ate whatever junk food my mother brought home to mask my feelings of being alone. The cabinets were always filled with cakes, cookies, chips, and candy, and the freezer always had plenty of irresistible chocolate marshmallow ice cream. Whenever I was depressed, which was quite often, I would binge on junk food.

To add insult to injury, my mother's favorite meal to make for us was Hamburger Helper. Yep, straight from the box to the pan; just add the meat. She was a single mom with no time to cook, so her meals were quick and unhealthy. Once a week, we were treated to tasty Kentucky Fried Chicken meals that consisted of very little chicken meat inside the greasy fried coating, mashed potatoes smothered in thick gravy, corn, and a buttered biscuit. Can someone say *heart attack waiting to happen?*

When Mom was inspired to spend a little more time in the kitchen, she created either a hot dog stew, a "Meat-Za Pie," or a fish stick casserole, which were simple recipes containing a bit of protein, pasta or rice, and lots of cheese. To her credit, she did make a mean lasagna, but I wouldn't consider her food choices healthy by any means.

When I got active in theater in my twenties, the weight started coming off. I gained confidence by being on stage doing what I loved. I learned what I needed to know about making healthier food choices by reading books and experimenting on myself, but my sweet tooth never left me, and I would find myself putting weight on over the holidays and on vacation. The main difference between my childhood and now is I know how to get rid of extra weight through mindful food choices and exercising as much as possible.

In 2019, I decided I wanted to keep my weight stable through tempting situations and I didn't want to diet, so I joined the Noom program. It's a holistic approach that incorporates the physical, mental, and spiritual aspects of being healthy and in shape. It focuses on awareness of the main questions: why, how, when, what, and how much are you eating.

The Noom program of intentional eating is where I learned and ingested my first set of M&Ms: mindfulness and moderation. I began to control my actions and learned how to connect my thoughts to my choices and subsequent actions. I finally understood that no foods were off limits and I didn't need to deprive myself of the sugary sweets I craved as long as I ate them in moderation and was mindful of why I was indulging.

Once I was aware of the psychology behind my eating habits, I was able to make changes and get back on the wagon more easily if I fell off. If you're an emotional eater and can relate to my story, I strongly suggest you check out Noom. It's a fun app that only takes five to ten minutes every day, and you learn empowering new habits and become aware of your choices.

Just so you know, I'm not a representative of Noom, nor do I make any commission by suggesting it. I'm simply telling you what worked for me in hopes that it'll work for you if you need it. Other diet programs out there like Weight Watchers and NutriSystem will also be effective if you do the work. Noom just happened to be an enjoyable little app, so I looked forward to doing the short lessons every day while I watched the numbers on the scale go down.

Let's open up your bag of M&Ms again because there's still one last morsel inside. This M is the concept of Miracles. Albert Einstein said, "There are two ways to live your life. One is as though nothing is a miracle. The other is as though everything is a miracle." Your life is truly a miracle; just that you're breathing and reading this book right now is a phenomenon. You are a magical miracle of nature.

We don't normally pay attention to what goes on behind the scenes in our bodies, but every organ, every bodily system, and every cell knows exactly what to do to keep us alive.

Whether you believe you are a part of the Divine Consciousness that created the planets, stars, and galaxies, or you believe everything is random and you're here for no reason or purpose, you can't deny your body is a magical wonder. Sure, people get sick and have chronic illnesses to deal with, but as long as we're able to breathe, and do whatever we can to keep breathing via healthy habits or medications, if you take care of your body, it will take care of you. It knows what you need, and it's really good at keeping you on this planet. Take a moment to be grateful for your amazing body. If you're not fully functioning, thank the parts of you that are working properly that allow you to live your life.

One of the most inspirational speakers I've ever heard, who gave me a hefty dose of motivation, is Nick Vujicic. Vujicic came out of the womb with a rare congenital disorder that left him without legs and arms. Despite his disabilities, his parents didn't over-pamper him; instead, they let him figure out how to function on his own. He found ways to maneuver through life and learned how to do everything able-bodied people could do. At the age of seventeen, he became a motivational speaker and continues to inspire people with his story. I encourage you to google him and watch some of his videos. When someone with no limbs hops around a stage and tells you that you can do anything you want, you can't help but believe it and be inspired to make things happen in your own life.

To recap the last two chapters, to increase your confidence, you need to nurture your body, mind, and spirit. Start adding new habits to your daily routine that serve you and keep you peaceful and motivated. Whether you begin a new morning routine, incorporate meditation into your day, begin a new exercise regime, practice mindfulness about what you eat, or use music to soothe your soul, you get to decide which tools works best for you. Try out each one and see how it goes. Find the techniques you enjoy so you'll do them every day until they're automatic. As they say in show biz, if it works, keep it in the act. As you continue to evolve and grow, you'll end up tweaking your habits to accommodate your ever-changing needs. On that note, it's time to take out your journal because we want to zone in on your current habits, decide what stays, what goes, and what new habits you need to create.

Ask yourself the following questions and write down your answers:

1. What habits do I need to break to get ahead?

2. What new habits will I create to move me forward?

3. What do I need to do differently?

4. Am I committed to breaking old habits and making new ones?

Take strides daily to make these changes so your habits will work in your favor instead of leading you into a pattern of self-sabotage. Remember that it takes a minimum of two months to create and reinforce new habits, so keep track of when you start something new and keep going with it until it happens naturally for you, like brushing your teeth at night.

Here are a few action steps to keep you inspired.

Step 1: Create a music playlist of ten to twenty songs that make you feel good and/or motivate you to dance. Listen to them often because the point is to live fully in the moment and enjoy your life. Have fun with this!

Step 2: Subscribe to inspirational podcasts you can listen to whenever you have a free moment to help keep you on track in developing confidence. Here are a few I personally listen to and recommend.

- *The School of Greatness* with Lewis Howes. In this top-ranked self-development podcast, a former pro athlete turned lifestyle entrepreneur interviews successful people from all walks of life. They share their tips to help you *unlock your inner greatness and live your best life*. It's informative, inspirational, and motivational, so I highly recommend giving it a listen.

- *Achieve Your Goals* with Hal Elrod. Here you'll find empowering information and interviews providing you with practical advice and methods to achieve your goals and dreams.

- *Expanded* with Lacy Phillips encompasses the topics of neuroscience, psychology, epigenetics, energetics, and expanding past your limiting subconscious beliefs. Here you'll find interviews with experts in their fields, thought leaders, spiritual teachers, scientists, and those who have achieved their dreams using various techniques.

- *Dear Gabby* hosted by international speaker and #1 *New York Times* bestselling author Gabrielle Bernstein. I first discovered Gabby's teachings when I read her book *The Universe Has Your Back*, which resonated deeply with me. I was thrilled that she decided to launch her weekly podcast in 2021. In addition to sharing her nuggets of wisdom, she has interesting conversations with inspirational leaders about personal growth and spirituality and does live one-on-one coaching for her listeners. As a spiritual seeker, I recommend this podcast gem if you're looking to dive more deeply into your spiritual practices to help transform your life.

Tons of motivational speakers and teachers are at your fingertips, so find the ones who appeal to and inspire you to keep going full steam ahead on your path. Knowledge is power.

In the next chapter, we'll learn yet another technique for becoming your best self: *Visualization*. It's the process of imagining your ideal future and envisioning yourself living out the life of your dreams. Want to *see* the future? Read on!

CHAPTER 7

YOUR FUTURE SELF

"Whatever the mind can conceive and believe,
the mind can achieve."

— *Napoleon Hill*

Be careful what you think and say. Your thoughts and words create your beliefs, and your subconscious acts on them because it doesn't judge and only listens to the information you feed it. You become what you think about. A powerful tool you can use to achieve the life of your dreams is based on this principle. It's a technique called visualization which utilizes your imagination. When you focus on what you want, while feeling the joy and jubilation of already having it, you can bring whatever it is into your life. The simple act of envisioning your future desires as if they are already happening will put you into a higher vibrational state, which then transmits out to the Universe. Remember how we talked about the fact that you are a vibrational being? Because of this, you can use the technique of visualization as a way of manifesting the things you want into your life.

All you need to do is create a vision of where you want to be. For instance, if your dream is to be a successful actress, feel yourself walking down a red carpet surrounded by paparazzi. If you're looking for a high-level executive position, see yourself sitting in your spacious, open, and airy office signing important documents and see your executive title on the corporate stationary. Whatever your soul is calling for you to do or you wish to do at a higher level, let your thoughts and imagination show you how it feels to already be there. Let the confident, joyful side of you relish the achievements you've made (in this new future). Instead of thinking to yourself, "I'll believe it when I see it," think, "I'll see it when I believe it!"

When you start visualizing what your ideal life will look like, you'll notice that life will present opportunities and the people needed to help you move along. Start believing in your dreams and the Universe will conspire to give you everything and everyone you need to get there.

Ask yourself these two questions: *What's the best that can happen to me? How do I want my life to go?* To give power to your dreams, visualize everything about this new future. Where are you? What are you doing? Notice the sights, sounds, and smells around you. Who is there with you? How much money do you have in the bank? How are you giving back? How has your life changed? Visualize every form of abundance you can think of in all aspects of your future life.

Take a look back at the wish list you created in Chapter 2. Close your eyes and visualize it all coming true. Create a movie in your mind of what your future self has become. Doesn't that feel amazing and exciting? You deserve all of this, so believe you're going to have it. Be patient knowing you *will* have it when the time is right.

For me, it was about performing on bigger stages and touching more people through the magic of music. I would close my eyes and feel myself on those bigger stages. I would see myself in a flab-free body. I would feel the elation and joy of knowing I was exactly where I wanted to be at that stage. I never gave up the quest. And I did play on those bigger stages.

I continued to visualize what I wanted next. Writing this book wasn't part of my initial dream, but I knew that when an inner calling strikes, it's a cue to act. This endeavor was yet another way for me to affect others' lives in a positive way. And while I was writing the book, another calling showed up that prompted me to become a transformational life coach, which allowed me to help others beyond this book!

Life is so much richer when you're in tune with your purpose and know what you want to contribute to the world. As long as you're continually finding ways to grow, your life will be that much more fulfilling. Keep in mind that dreams may change throughout your life, and that's perfectly fine as long as you're staying true to yourself and using your innate gifts.

"Once you make a decision, the Universe conspires to make it happen."

— Ralph Waldo Emerson

Have you ever heard of the Law of Attraction (LOA)? Many people have heard about it through the movie *The Secret*, but people around the world have been using this Universal law to their benefit for a long time. The LOA is simply the ability to attract whatever we focus on. According to Wikipedia, the concept originates from various philosophical and religious traditions and was inspired by Hermeticism, New England transcendentalism, specific verses from the Bible, and Hinduism.

However, the LOA as we understand it today started in 1906 when author William Walker Atkinson released his book, *Thought Vibration or the Law of Attraction in the Thought World*, which described the concepts of vibrations and manifestation. Since we are vibrational beings, we attract the vibrations we're putting out.

One caveat, though—you must believe you are worthy and deserving of receiving everything you're asking for! Your life reflects your vibrational patterns of thought, so use the power of your thoughts to serve you. Reach for your *feel-good* dreams and enjoy the exhilaration of your new life as future you. The Universe will bring you what you're asking for if you believe it, envision it, and feel it. It's a matter of tapping into and trusting the invisible nature of our world. What you think about expands, so focus your thoughts on the beautiful life that awaits you. You'll notice how things will begin to shift as you watch the magic that enfolds.

Many teachers speak about visualization techniques. One proponent of this technique is Mike Dooley, a metaphysical teacher and the bestselling author of many acclaimed books about living your best life. He offers online classes and has a daily newsletter called *Notes from the Universe*, which I personally receive in my inbox as a source of inspiration every day. I encourage you to do the same because it will inspire you to keep dreaming. You can find the link here: www.tut.com.

Dooley has many memorable quotes to prod you into your future happiness. He asserts, "Wherever your thoughts can go, you can go." He also said, "It may seem a bit backward for some, but the first step one might take toward rearranging the present circumstances of their life is to stop dwelling upon the present circumstances of their life." Know that your thoughts and your imagination are powerful, especially when you choose to use them to visualize the life you crave.

An enlightening book written about this topic is Wayne Dyer's *How to Get What You Really, Really, Really Want*. In it, he mentions the four steps necessary for achieving your desires. It starts with a wish. You simply start out thinking about what you want and write down or say the words, "I wish…."

Note that you already completed step one of this process when you wrote down your wish list in Chapter 2, but if you haven't done that yet, it's in your best interest to get clarity on what you want your life to look like.

In step two, you decide whether your wish is a true desire. Is it something that burns deep within you and that you know you must have to feel fulfilled? What is your inner being telling you? If your wish is a true desire, ask your Higher Power to help you create your deepest desires.

Step three is when you state and confirm you intend to achieve your desired life. With no doubt in your mind, start by saying, "I will…." By switching from wishing to desiring to stating that you *will* create what you want in your life, it will show up for you. Just like the whispering voice in the movie *Field of Dreams* telling Kevin Costner,

"If you build it, he will come," internally whisper to yourself that you are building your dream life and it, too, will come your way.

The fourth and final step is important to making it happen. It is staying committed. You know what you want, and you know you must have it to live your fullest life. You've asked God (or whatever you label that higher energy) for it zestfully, and you expect it to happen. But you have to stay passionate about it even when it doesn't seem like anything is changing. If you come across naysayers trying to squash your dreams, don't listen to them. This is your life, not theirs, so stay true to yourself and to your quest. Keep visualizing where you want to be and who you want to become.

Another technique you can use to visualize is a Vision Board. I have an actress friend I've known for decades who was doing off-off Broadway shows when we first met. She had a vision board in her apartment. She knew exactly where she wanted to be and what she wanted to achieve, and she knew she had the goods to get there. Andrea Sooch is now a successful actress who has appeared in major roles on network TV and in films. Not only did she achieve what she set out to do, but she also branched out into another line of work that was equally as fulfilling to her soul.

Along with acting, Andrea is now a licensed social worker, specializing in helping people through the power of drama therapy. She continues to learn, grow, and share her wisdom and positivity with the world. I can't think of a better example of someone who stayed focused on her dreams, believed in herself, and continued to challenge herself while helping others along the way.

You can create your own vision board by cutting out pictures and images of people, things, or experiences similar to what you want from magazines and arranging them on a cork or poster board. You can also add sayings, affirmations, or concepts alongside them. For instance, on my original board, I had the following images:

- Places I wanted to visit next to the word *travel.*

- A girl in a yoga pose with the word *connecting.*

- A girl joyfully standing on a scale with her arms raised in a success pose next to the word *goals.*

- A hand with a stack of money in it along with the affirmation, "*Money comes to me doing that which I love.*"

Interspersed among these pictures, I also had the words *success, love, laughter, creativity,* and *health.* Our lives are constantly changing, and so are our desires, so your vision board will continue to change. There are also online apps you can use to create your boards. A search on Google or on your app store will lead you to sites like Canva, PicMonkey, Mind Movies, and DreamItAlive.

Many teachers use and recommend visualization to help create your new life. Mindset and behavior expert John Assaraf created an extremely helpful template called the *Exceptional Life Blueprint.* With it, you can insert pictures and vision statements that cover your values, purpose, and goals. One of the template pages prompts you to create the new story of your future and write it down in the present tense. He suggests either reading it every day or making a recording of it and keeping it on your phone to listen to daily. As stated previously, the subconscious doesn't know what's real or what's actually happening now, so the key is consistently to feed it with the life story you wish to create.

Another very comprehensive program is *Lifebook* by Jon and Missy Butcher. It can be found at Mindvalley.com. This program consists of eighteen hours of training over a six-week period, in which you dive deeply into all aspects of your life and end up with a very detailed vision of your dream life.

Mary Morrissey, creator of the Dreambuilder Life Coaching program, also uses visualization as an action step in achieving your most abundant life. She often says, "Everything happens twice, once in thought and once in form." She bases her teachings upon the spiritual nature of who we are as vibrational beings and states, "The frequency you are tuned to determines your destiny." Essentially, what we think, we become, since the Universe reacts to our frequencies. She uses the analogy of how each channel on TV or radio has a certain frequency, so you need to select the right channel to get what you're looking for. You're not going to find heavy metal music on a country music station, nor will you see soap operas on a sports channel. You have to tune directly into the station you're looking for. Similarly, you have to streamline your wishes vibrationally and stay focused on your vision for your life story.

"Be careful what you wish for, lest it come true."

— Aesop

Equally important as focusing on what you want is being conscious of your thoughts about what you don't want. You now know that what you focus on expands and is attracted into your life, so if you're focusing on what's missing, you're going to attract more of the same. For this reason, stay mindful of your thoughts and focus your attention on your dreams, instead of concentrating on what you lack. Listen to the voices of discontent, lack, and longing, and use them to lead you to where you'd rather be, but then leave them behind; keep your thoughts on your new focal point, which is your soon-to-be joyful and abundant life.

The best way to create more abundance, as we touched on earlier, is to live gratefully. Take an inventory of all the things going right for you in this moment. Think of your loved ones, your friends, and that you have a place to live and food on your table. The more you are grateful for, the more you'll have to be grateful for. Mary Morrissey points out, "Gratitude is a magnet for what we would love more of and is the feeling tone that is harmonious with the experience of abundance." Remember, that you are a vibrational being, and you create your vibrational state with your thoughts.

As you make plans for your future, leave room to be flexible when life throws you opportunities. Keep in mind that your *Higher Self* dreams bigger dreams than you could ever imagine, and life can also throw you curve balls from time to time. For instance, at the beginning of 2020, I labeled my morning journal "2020! A year of personal growth and new experiences!" I could not have known the world was going to change so drastically or how different those new experiences would be. Not only did I grow exponentially from all the spiritual and self-help information I took in during the pandemic, but this book was just a pipe dream before the downtime the pandemic brought gave me time to write it. With that, my life changed dramatically in a way I never would have expected. So, I suggest you **stay open to the positivity that may be hidden within the turmoil.**

> *"All our dreams can come true if we have the courage to pursue them."*
>
> — Walt Disney

To live in your purpose and on purpose, you have to be continually mindful of the bigger questions. Why are you here? What is your reason for being on this planet? What do you intend to do with your life? These are the very questions that will prod you along on a peaceful and successful journey. You've already taken time to explore these facets of yourself in previous chapters, and you have written down your wish list of things you want to have, be, and do. You know how to visualize and imagine them as if they're already happening, but there's another step to obtaining your dreams: living with intention.

Living mindfully and with intention involves knowing the deeper meaning for your life and reminding yourself of your bigger picture. It's a process of being aware of *why* you're taking steps to create your reality. In the acting world, actors usually ask the director, "What's my motivation?" because they need to know the reason they're saying or doing something. As the actor in your own life, you need to ask yourself that same question. What's the purpose or goal behind your actions? Why do you want what you want? What's the driving force behind your desires?

Obviously, you long for all of the material things on your wish list, such as your dream house or that brand new, self-driving Tesla Model 3 you've been eyeing simply because you're human. Most people probably aspire to having a healthy bank account, consisting of ample available cash, long-term savings, and successful growth stocks, but what does that money signify for you? For me, it equates to freedom because it allows me to travel, have fun adventures and experiences, buy gifts for family and friends, donate to my favorite charities, and give back to the world, all without putting a strain on my personal finances.

What does the word *wealth* mean to you? Do you want to be a millionaire? Why? Why do you want to be healthy? Close your eyes, connect to your inner awareness, and ask yourself these questions. Listen for the answers. When you get the inner message, open your eyes and write down what you heard so you know the reasons behind your bigger vision. And once you've written them down, visualize your ideal story again, and let the feelings of excitement, peace, and satisfaction take over your body. You now have your ultimate motivation that comes straight from your soul. If you just go through your days struggling to get things done without a sense of intention or purpose, you'll be denying what could be your deepest and most fulfilling moments.

In all aspects of life, keep in mind what's driving your actions by silently asking the questions, "Why am I doing this? Is this action empowering me to live a better life?" And while you're in *silent mode*, don't forget to tap into the higher part of yourself to listen for guidance. All of your answers are within, so stay connected to your inner voice. In the words of Maria Erving, author of *Energy Awareness*, "Don't go against your inner knowing. Just don't. Trust yourself." Tapping into your intuition and inner guidance will give you full-on, life-changing effects. And remember, everything starts with a thought. Intentional thoughts lead to taking necessary actions to make life happier and more productive.

> *"If you can visualize a goal for yourself, you have the inherent ability to make that dream a reality. All you need to do is act on it."*
>
> *— Jack Canfield*

There's one final factor necessary for achieving your desires. Your intentions and feelings are powerful, but they can't work without action. Visualization is an amazing tool for making things happen, but you still need to put in the effort to plan and create change. If you're not sure how to get where you want to be, keep in mind that you're not alone on your quest. You're co-creating with the greatest power and source of knowledge in the Universe, and it dwells inside of you.

You don't need to know *how* it's all going to come together because your inner awareness knows exactly which opportunities are meant to come your way to guide you on your path. It will bring you the right people to assist you, and it will continually prod you toward your dreams and inspire you with Divine guidance. It might prompt you to take classes or learn from people who have been in your shoes and know how to fast-track your process. You might be drawn to read certain books or watch videos or webinars, or out of the blue, you find yourself having *light bulb moments* of inspiration where ideas seem to flow to you.

If you stay connected to your inner awareness and truly listen to its guidance, your life will progress with more ease. Remember, the word *inspiration* is derived from the words *in-spirit*, which is the state that will best serve you.

For my science friends, think of it as being in tune with your vibrational, energetic life force. And if you prefer to go it alone without the help of any spiritual assistance, notice how that's working for you. Something tells me that if you're reading this book, you're looking for help and guidance. Again, I'm not writing to persuade anyone about my beliefs. I encourage you to stay true to yourself. There's no right or wrong way to discover your way to your best life. Find what works for you, and stick with it. I'm simply sharing what I've found to be invaluable to turning my life around in hopes that it will be helpful to you too. My advice is to look inward for the answers to all your questions. The Higher Intelligence inside of you knows what's best for you.

"When we realize our magnificence and live in our true nature of love, we'll synchronistically attract the right teacher, book, or spiritual philosophy at the right time!"

— Anita Moorjani

Have you ever experienced thinking about someone and then, out of the blue, they called you? Or perhaps you wanted to learn how to do something, and you instantly came across someone who knew how to do that very thing? Do you see posters or signs for things that might be meaningful to you and keep seeing them over and over again? Or maybe you open to a page in a book and find a sentence that seems to be speaking to you directly. You might consider these as random occurrences or merely coincidences, but they're much more than that. When you are aligned with your dreams and your visualizations, synchronicity happens. It's the invisible energy that is aligning the right people and resources in your life to help you along your path. It usually happens when you're open and ready to receive the information you need.

Albert Einstein said it perfectly: "Coincidence is God's way of remaining anonymous." It's a magical thing to experience these forms of assistance from the unseen. You don't need to micromanage your life. The more you live in harmony with your strong desires, the more you'll experience these miracle moments of guidance from the Universe.

It's interesting how life operates in terms of giving you signs. I purposely included thirteen chapters in this book because the numbers one and three have popped up for me my whole life, but more so this last year. Although I'm not into numerology, I had to look up these numbers; astonishingly, they represent creative self-expression, communication, progress, motivation, individuality, confidence, leadership, joy, optimism, happiness, ambition, growth, expansion, moving forward, and new beginnings. These are all facets of my life that have been front and center since I started writing. Coincidence? Highly doubtful. I believe it's reassurance from the Universe that I'm on the right track. Pay attention to recurring signs because they might be telling you something too.

Now let's practice the principles we talked about in this chapter by doing some writing exercises.

EXERCISE 1: VISUALIZE

As Mark Twain said, "Twenty years from now, you'll be more disappointed by the things you didn't do, than by the things you did."

In this exercise, you're going to envision what your ideal life will look like five years from now. What are you doing? Who are you with? How much money do you have? What kind of shape are you in? Where are you living? What are you experiencing? Begin by getting into a relaxed state and then put on your imagination cap. Be very specific with the details. If you're expecting to have an income of $100,000 five years from now, put that down instead of saying you want a lot of money. You're giving the Universe a detailed description of what you want so it can bring it into your life.

Once you're clear on your vision, write it all down in the present tense as if it's already happening. Start your sentences with "*I am...*" and soak it all in as you're writing it. Then say it out loud. Notice how that makes you feel. Is this the life you would really love? This feeling will direct your thoughts into creating your new reality. Read your vision statements every day until they sink into your subconscious.

Better yet, record your vision on your smartphone in your own voice so you can listen to it. When you create pictures in your mind and visualize your dreams, you'll see things begin to change and opportunities start opening up.

EXERCISE 2: YOUR ACTION PLAN

Begin by taking a few deep breaths and closing your eyes. Ask yourself what action steps you can take to move closer to your dreams.

Listen for the answers, and then write down ten things that come to mind. Once you have your list, start taking action one day at a time. Small steps forward lead to big changes, so stay consistent.

Now that you have a clear vision of your future self in mind, in the next chapter, we're going to discuss the importance of taking necessary daily action steps to move toward your dream and how procrastination and perfectionism can hold you back.

CHAPTER 8

GET INTO A GROOVE

*"All the world's a stage and most of
us are desperately unrehearsed."*

— *Seán O'Casey*

Some people are naturally born to sing. They just open their mouths and out comes a beautiful symphony of sound. I have a few ultra-talented singer friends who never took voice lessons, but unfortunately, I am not one of those people. As mentioned previously, my first love was dance, and I begged my mother to put me into dancing school. I never asked her for singing lessons, even though music was part of my healing process when my father left. Only when I started getting the leads in shows because I looked the part did I realize I was good enough to sing on a stage. In my early twenties, I started studying with an opera singer who taught me the fundamentals of singing correctly. She started me out with the basics of diaphragmatic breathing, along with doing numerous types of scales that made me stronger. As I got more and more experience, my voice developed. But even to this day, I have to work on my vocal skills and practice as much as I can.

My background was in musical theater, so when I crossed over into singing pop music, I was awful! The producer of the show literally took me to the side, asked me if I could hear myself, and then said my pitch was all over the place. I wasn't used to singing contemporary music at all, and it showed. He said I needed to practice and record myself so I could hear what I sounded like, and he added that if I didn't get better, he'd have to find a replacement. That was an eye-opener for me. I knew it was time to get serious about developing my skills if I wanted to stay in the game. During this time of working six nights a week, doing two Broadway-themed variety shows with costumes and choreography, as well as three dance sets between the shows, I worked really hard to get up to snuff. We had to drop some songs from the dance sets because I couldn't quite nail them stylistically, but my pitch improved dramatically. I eventually started working in the New York club date circuit singing with bands at private functions and corporate parties. To do this, I had to bump up my repertoire to include every style imaginable, and I hunkered down for months on end to get a working setlist of songs, ranging from current music to the hits from each decade. The learning process never ended because each party always had special requests, so I would need to learn new material. In the process, I kept honing my craft and continued to grow.

Ernest Hemingway said, "You must be prepared always without applause," and it's the truth. When it comes to having confidence in your abilities, the key is to practice, practice, practice! A writer writes, a singer sings, an artist creates art, an athlete does athletic drills, and people in business do their research in their field to up their game. Whatever it is you do, do it, and do it a lot! This will only serve you to get better and better and make you more marketable. If you're starting a business, take the time to learn the steps you need to take to get to where you want to be. Learn every facet of what you need to know to become successful. Be fearless and persistent in your efforts because they will pay off in time. *Your journey is a never-ending process of becoming better than you were.*

"Take back your power and claim 100% responsibility for your life."

— Jack Canfield

Jack Canfield encourages everyone to take full responsibility for their lives, and he incorporates all aspects of the mind-body-spirit connection into his teachings. Aside from meditation and being mindful of your thoughts, he states that the most essential factor for success is to take action to get to where you need to be. What steps are you taking to move toward the direction of your life's vision? Do you need to schedule more practice time? Do you need to spend more time researching the business end of your chosen profession? Do you need to learn new skills and gain new information? Do you need to learn how to promote your services or products? Whatever will propel you into forward motion, do it! Focus your energies on being the best of who you are.

Even the professionals still take time to work on their craft. I had the pleasure of opening up for recording artist Billy Gilman, who came to notoriety in 2000 with his hit single "One Voice" and whose debut album sold more than two million copies in the United States. He was also listed in the *Guinness Book of World Records* for being the youngest singer ever to reach #1 on the Billboard Top Country

Album charts. You may remember Billy from Season 11 of NBC's *The Voice* in 2016. To date, he's sold five million albums worldwide, and he has been given multiple awards and pure respect from the music industry. With a background like that, I was taken by surprise when he showed up to the gig with his vocal coach by his side and mentioned that he practiced daily to keep himself in tip-top shape for his performances. If you've never heard Billy sing, check him out on YouTube or go to his website. His voice is incredibly powerful, and he was jaw-dropping to watch in person. In November 2019, he came out with a song titled "Soldier." The catchy part of the song states, "I will keep fighting, 'cause baby I'm a soldier." This is exactly the headset you need to be in when you have a goal in mind. Keep fighting to reach for your dreams, and always keep in mind that practicing your craft is an essential part of getting there!

For more than ten years, I lived in a building on 43rd Street between 9th and 10th Avenue in New York City called Manhattan Plaza, just blocks away from the infamous Times Square. This government-subsidized building was opened in 1977 to help entertainers survive amid the city's rising rent costs. Alicia Keys was born here, Samuel Jackson was a security guard here, and it's the building where Larry David and Kenny Kramer of *Seinfeld* were neighbors. Numerous celebrities, musicians, actors, producers, directors, and artists came and went in this complex, and one of them lived in the apartment below mine. I noticed that almost every day, a trumpet player was practicing musical scales for about a half hour to an hour. He turned out to be renowned Russian jazz trumpet player Valery Ponomarev. When we first met in the building's shared laundry room, I told him I lived over his apartment, and he was nice enough to ask if his practicing was a disturbance. I didn't mind, and he didn't realize he was inspiring me to stay on top of my game just by witnessing how disciplined he was.

To power up your dreams, you need to power up your skills. Only you can make a difference in your own life, and to be the best you can be at your craft, you have to do the work. If you want to get better at something, practice daily and take action steps toward your goal and what's important to you. Honor your life and make yourself a priority.

"Perfectionism is the enemy of creation."

— John Updike

Fill in the blank…. "Practice makes _____." I'll bet you thought the last word was *perfect*, didn't you? Yes, that's the old adage, but truth be told, there is no such thing as perfection. We are ever-evolving and expanding to higher levels of being. However, if you're getting stuck in negative self-talk, telling yourself you're not good enough, it's time to change your thoughts, change your story, and let go of perfectionism. Zero in on your strengths, continue to build on them, and focus even harder on mastering your weaker points.

Never stop working on your craft, and always keep in mind that there is no final destination. You will never fully *get it done* because your life is a journey of becoming your best self. Give it your all, and always be gentle, patient, and kind to yourself as you travel along your path. As you sharpen your skills, you'll be making greater and greater progress. Behavior expert John Assaraf said, "Practice makes permanent." That's a great quote to keep in mind. The empowering habit of practicing consistently will not only upgrade your expertise but make you more confident and ready to take on your dreams full force.

I must admit that releasing the concept of imperfection has always been a constant struggle for me. I don't know if it's a blessing or a curse, but I've always been the type of person whose eyes immediately go to typos on a page and who notices minor imperfections that are meaningless when it comes to the bigger picture. There's a time and a place to nitpick, but not when it comes to causing yourself stress by casting unnecessary judgment on yourself. Although I've always tended to be very hard on myself and strive to be at my best on all occasions, my new and improved version has learned to relax into the flow of life and not stress over self-imposed expectations of perfection.

We are all *perfectly imperfect* as we build our own masterpieces, one step at a time. Even legendary songwriter Leonard Cohen knew there was no such thing as perfection when he wrote the lyrics to his song "Anthem" that stated: "There is a crack in everything. That's how the light gets in."

There's beauty in imperfection.

It allows us to keep improving and growing. On that note, I advise you to strive to be your best but accept that imperfection is perfectly okay! As you keep practicing your craft, you're going to step into your power and become confident that you can do anything you choose to do.

You're a work in progress, just like we all are. Know that every step you take forward will guide you to your highest potential.

I'd like to take a moment to address something that could easily get in your way and thwart your progress. It shows up in the form of delay and distraction and is called procrastination. We all do it now and then. But when we allow it to happen, it doesn't serve us in the least. American entrepreneur Jim Rohn said, "We must all suffer from one of two pains: the pain of discipline or the pain of regret. The difference is discipline weighs ounces while regret weighs tons."

Think about that for a second. If you don't stick to your new habit of practicing, what will it cost you years down the road? When you procrastinate, you find reasons not to get started, lose your focus, and waste your energy doing things that aren't purposeful or productive. In the long run, it will sabotage your confidence, cause you more stress and frustration, make you less motivated, and take you away from your bigger vision.

Habitual procrastination is a slow process of letting yourself down and stopping you from becoming your best self. The next time you feel like putting a task off until tomorrow, resist the urge, and instead, give yourself a pep talk about why you need to act. You're reading this book to move out of self-defeating ways, and this is a big part of the equation. Do it now. Do it now. Do it now!

A great way to stay on track is to schedule practice days on your calendar. Set a specific time you will hunker down and practice. What gets scheduled, gets done. Remember that only you can make your life beautiful, and you do that by the choices you make. Choose to be tenacious and disciplined. After that, all you need to do is show up fully as you are and accept that you are perfect just as you are. Embrace that notion and give yourself a big hug.

Let's get to work.

EXERCISE

Open up your datebook and schedule in the days and times you're going to practice or work on your skills in the upcoming week. Continue to do this weekly so you can work around all of the other things you have planned each week. Whether it's fifteen minutes or an hour, find a slot of time when you can focus solely on developing your craft or your business without distractions. Turn off your phone, tell your family you need some alone time, and get it done. Baby steps lead to giant leaps, and the ensuing competence you achieve will lead to full-on confidence.

Your only real job is to be authentically yourself. In the next chapter, we'll dive more deeply into how embracing every aspect of your uniqueness is essential to your progress.

CHAPTER 9

JUST BE YOU

"Wanting to be someone else is a waste of who you are."

— Kurt Cobain

"You're too quirky for commercials. You don't fit into any of the formula molds." In my late twenties, I heard these words when I had a one-on-one interview with a casting director. Every time I auditioned for a commercial, I was told I was too ethnic looking, not blonde, not young enough, not tall enough, not "business looking," not *anything* enough to get commercial work. But that didn't stop me from going to auditions. I did eventually stop going because I realized I didn't enjoy acting as much as I loved singing and dancing, and I wanted to focus on my true passions.

The only acting job I was almost considered for was on the soap opera *All My Children,* but unfortunately, they were looking for someone edgy and on the nasty side, and my general nature is just the opposite. The casting director had a brief conversation with me and didn't ask me to stay. She said I was too nice. I have to say that was the first time that character trait worked against me. We can only be who we are—or as Popeye says, "I yam what I yam."

It took me a long time to discover I was stressing myself out by listening to others who thought I should be a certain way. I continually compared myself to other artists and didn't acknowledge or accept the uniqueness of who I was. I came to learn that in the buffet of life, we each have unique gifts and abilities to bring to the table. If someone doesn't like our *dish*, it doesn't mean there's something wrong with it. It just means their taste buds prefer a different flavor. You brought a delicious and healthy baked chicken, and they were looking for breaded fried chicken. They passed on your home-cooked chicken because it didn't appeal to them, but others dug right in.

Similarly, what others think of you is not a reflection of who you are or how good you are at what you do. Once I came to terms with this concept, I was able to remain peaceful if I didn't get a callback from an audition I thought I did well on. I didn't bombard my brain with thoughts of why I didn't hear from them. I simply accepted that it wasn't meant to be part of my path and moved on to something else. The best we can do is show up in the world as our true selves and have the confidence to know that if it's meant to be for us, it will be.

Just show up and do you!

Accepting and embracing every aspect of yourself may be new to you. It requires being mindful of your self-talk and taking persistent action to change those negative thoughts into positive affirmations about how amazing you are. Reciting affirmations daily will condition you to love who you are, as you are. At first, you may feel reluctant to do your affirmations because it feels fake, but the more you become aware of your disempowering thoughts and change them around while affirming the new empowering ones, the more self-confidence you'll develop.

As noted previously, when you state your positive affirmations with energy and passion, you'll be faking it so well that you'll start to believe it. Eventually, you'll accept yourself wholeheartedly and will be quick to notice any thoughts that simply aren't true. This includes what you consider to be your quirks and your flaws. To be human is to have a combination of strengths and weaknesses—it's all a part of who we are. If you feel you can be or do better at certain things, then work on it, but again, be gentle and kind with yourself and learn how to be your own best friend.

Think about that last part for a second. If your best friend was knocking themselves down because they didn't feel good enough, or smart enough, or *anything* enough, what would you tell them? My guess is you'd tell them they're putting themselves down needlessly and they have so much to offer. You'd remind them about all of their wonderful qualities and encourage them to live fearlessly and to love and believe in themselves. You'd be feeding their thoughts of how competent they are and inspiring them to get out of their own head. This is exactly what you need to be doing for yourself.

Stop judging yourself so harshly and being your own worst critic. It's okay to feel emotional when things don't go the way you had hoped, but don't remain there too long. Love yourself so unconditionally that nothing can stop you. Keep reminding yourself of your greatness and stay on course, taking action to joyfully become better and better at doing what you love to do. Proceed confidently in the world and the world will give you more and more opportunities to grow, expand, and thrive.

"Don't compare your life to others.
There's no comparison between the sun and the moon;
they just shine when it's their time."

— Unknown

When I was younger, one of my favorite shows was *The Brady Bunch*. I was obsessed and infatuated with Marsha Brady and wanted to be just like her. She was the epitome of perfection, and I felt completely inferior to her in all ways. Like my Barbie Dolls growing up, Marsha had the perfect body, perfect hair, a perfect outgoing personality, and was perfectly popular. In my young eyes, I couldn't hold a candle to her. I didn't realize that my already defeated thought patterns were being reinforced by constantly comparing my life to this unflawed TV character. I hadn't yet discovered that I was born with my own unique beauty and personality traits that remained hidden due to my feelings of inferiority. And I certainly didn't know I came to this lifetime fully equipped with everything I would ever need inside of me.

In the early 1990s, I had the pleasure of meeting singer-songwriter Idina Menzel on a showcase for a wedding band agency we both worked in. She was sweet as pie and told me she was in rehearsals for an off-Broadway show called *Rent*. Months later, on the night before its premiere, the show's creator, Jonathan Larsen, died. The show became an instant sensation and Idina's career took off. In no time, she was catapulted to Broadway to play Elphaba, the Wicked Witch of the West in the show *Wicked*, followed by numerous celebrity galas, awards, notoriety, and in the process, she became a superstar—

the world knew her name (except John Travolta, that is). I couldn't help but ask the Universe, "When is it going to be my turn?"

I was really happy for Idina, but I wanted to have my own glamorous show biz life. I had a choice to make. Did I want to keep comparing my life to someone else's or keep moving forward trusting that life would give me what I needed the most? Did I want to be a celebrity because I wanted attention or because I had a pure intention to keep doing what I loved? Since I felt ignored as a child, I would have to say my intentions were partly based on subconscious needs at first, but I eventually came to realize one of my essential needs is to do what I love and make a living at it.

It took me almost a lifetime to stop comparing myself to others. Once I stopped doing it, my confidence increased dramatically, and I began believing in and embracing what was exclusively and innately in me. I came to know that life doesn't happen *to* us, but *for* us. As I strengthened my spiritual connection, I realized there's an energy inside each of us that comes from a higher energy source. Although we're born with different physical characteristics, personalities, and talents, we're still part of the Divine oneness.

Michael Jordan might not have coined this phrase, nor did one of my favorite bandleaders, but it rings true that "There's no I in team." In life itself, we are all part of a human spiritual family. Once we recognize this, we can relinquish any negative energy spent on comparing ourselves to others. Like a snowflake, we come into this life with our very own thumbprint and design. Let go of the need to prove yourself to anyone else. You have your own voice and your own path, and they have theirs. Be at peace with that thought. Some people will always be farther along in their careers than you are, and others will be far behind on their journey.

Since each of us is born with unique gifts, we need not feel superior or inferior to anyone. We're all entitled to live life on our own terms. We don't need to trample over anyone in the process. Instead of choosing to feel inadequate when someone's strengths are our weaknesses, learn from them. Honor their talents with respect and celebrate where they are on their journey, knowing that you, too, can teach someone else who needs more of what you have.

Keep celebrating who you are as you celebrate others. In the words of Roy T. Bennett, author of *The Light in The Heart*, "Be brave enough to live the life of your dreams according to your vision and purpose instead of the expectations and opinions of others."

Throughout my twenties and thirties, I didn't realize I was living with a sense of lack instead of a sense of abundance because that's all I ever knew. I didn't know there was enough for everyone, and I always felt like my career was one big competitive game. Now I know there's no need to be jealous of others' accomplishments. Jealousy serves no purpose; it only keeps us stuck and feeling defeated. If you're still in the comparison phase like I was, I encourage you to do yourself a favor and concentrate on running your own race doing what you do best—genuinely being *you*. Mary Morrissey said, "You're here to create, not to compete." Value yourself and your journey through this life by acknowledging that no one can offer what you are here to share with the world. Accept your *"enoughness."* You're here to live your happiest and most fulfilling life. Cradle yourself in love and the joy of becoming who you were meant to be.

Similarly, give up the need for others' approval. As a people-pleaser for the majority of my life, I put others' opinions in front of my own for a long time. To avoid confrontation, I wouldn't speak what was on my mind. I would be *nice* and tell people what I thought they wanted to hear.

I wasn't living authentically.

I sacrificed who I was to be accepted and liked. It took a long time to take my mask off and reveal my true self. To get to that point, I needed to develop self-confidence and face my fears of speaking up for myself. I learned I could be honest with people and still maintain those relationships. I also learned some people enjoy being argumentative—it's their comfort zone. I know my limits now, and if something turns into a debate where the other person isn't open-minded, I try to lead the conversation to a different topic. I now know when to gracefully bow out of a conversation that negatively affects my peace. If someone can't be respectful and decent, it's out of my control. They are who they are, and I have a choice about how to respond to them.

Again, I'm always trying to stay in the higher energies of peace, joy, and positivity. If you find yourself in a position where you're getting into a heated conversation and it has stopped being productive, it's to your benefit to respectfully withdraw. Choose peace, and choose to serve your soul. Do your best to keep negative energy and toxicity out of your life. In the words of George Bernard Shaw, "Never wrestle with pigs. You both get dirty, and the pig likes it."

Negative people take others down with them, so limit your exposure to this type of energy and always choose to keep your composure and stay calm. For all of my fellow *Seinfeld* fans, do you remember the episode where George Costanza's father's therapist told him to use the phrase *Serenity Now*? Use a catch phrase similar to that if you need it. Rid yourself of the tension and shake it off. Make it a point to surround yourself with as many successful, positive, happy, and fulfilled people as you can. These self-actualized individuals have developed their own success principles that can help you along and keep you inspired.

One of my favorite TV shows is Oprah Winfrey's *Super Soul Sunday* where she interviews celebrities, authors, spiritual thinkers, and people who have made a positive difference in the world. All of them share the lessons and moments of enlightenment they've experienced. You can also hear Winfrey's personal selection of these interviews on the Super Soul podcast if you don't subscribe to the Discovery+ channel where she airs her show.

When Winfrey first premiered the show in 2011, she sent everyone interested in watching a free journal to take notes. I filled it up in no time and had to buy another notebook because I learned so much from the program and its guests. Here are just a few quotes that stuck out for me in the series of interviews Winfrey conducted:

"You can live your life out of your circumstances, or you can live your life out of your vision. The risk is standing still."

— Barbara Brown Taylor, Preacher, Professor, Author, and Theologian

"The only way to success is your own imagination."

— *Shonda Rhimes, Author of* Year of Yes: How to Dance It
Out, Stand In the Sun, *and* Be Your Own Person

"Don't be afraid of change and stay out of your own way."

— *Patti LaBelle, Legendary Singer*

*"When your personality comes to serve the energy of
your soul, that is authentic power."*

— *Gary Zukav, Author of* The Seat of the Soul

*"You will never rise any higher than the way you see yourself.
You have a choice to change your story. Be clear about
what you want, not what you settle for."*

— *Pastor Joel Osteen, Televangelist*

Many self-aware, self-actualized souls who have found wisdom
through their experiences walk among us. Listen to what they
have to say; their words may resonate with you and motivate or
inspire you.

John Lennon had the best message of all time when he wrote, "All
You Need Is Love." Yes! Love makes the world go 'round, and basically, love is all that truly matters. In the musical *Rent*, one song

alludes to the fact that we each have 525,600 minutes to live out our lives each year, and we should try to measure our lives by how much love we have in that year.

To move gracefully through the world, do your best to always keep love in your heart. That means loving yourself, loving others, and loving your life. At the Tony Awards in 2016, Lin-Manuel Miranda, creator of the Broadway smash *Hamilton*, won the award for Best Score. At the end of his emotional and touching acceptance speech, he said, "Love is love is love is love is love is love is love is love cannot be killed or swept aside." I couldn't agree more. Love is all there is.

At the top of the list is self-love. To love others, you need to fully embrace all aspects of yourself. Eliminate self-criticism, and instead, practice self-compassion. Whenever you catch yourself in the act of negative self-talk, mentally say to those thoughts, *I hear you, but what you're saying is a lie. You better get your facts straight. Let me tell you the truth....* And then do your affirmations. Always honor who you really are and give yourself a hefty dose of tender loving care because you deserve it. Once you get the hang of giving yourself hugs, comforting words, and deserved praise, you'll undoubtedly see a shift in the way you walk through the world.

When it comes to how you interact with others, approach everyone you meet with respect and understanding. If they seem ornery or nasty, try to be kind anyway. You aren't walking in their shoes and have no idea what kind of mental or emotional baggage they're carrying around. Everyone needs to feel heard, loved, and acknowledged, so listen to what people say instead of thinking about what you'll say next.

We are diverse individuals, and our viewpoints reflect the differences. Everyone is entitled to be who they are and uniquely express themselves. By trying to win them over to your way of being or thinking, you invalidate them. That's not love; that's just your ego talking.

If someone tells you you're wrong because they have a different opinion, speak what's on your mind, but if things get too intense and it's causing you to lose your peace, bow out. If the disagreement is with a friend, don't let the disagreement ruin your friendship. Keep love in your heart at all times. Wayne Dyer said, "It's better to be kind than to be right." In other words, always try to take the high road. If a relationship turns toxic, you'll need to love that person from afar. Remember always that one of the ways to a happy life is to choose peace.

One thing that always stuck with me during challenging relationships is that "Hurt people hurt people." If someone was damaged in their childhood and hasn't worked through it and released those wounds, they carry the pain, anger, and hurt with them into their relationships. Even though they're adults, they may still feel a need to prove that they're lovable, worthy, and worth listening to.

In one of my own long-term relationships, my partner and I both came from dysfunctional families, so it was an extremely bumpy ride. Ironically, my ex turned out to be my greatest teacher. If I hadn't experienced that much love for someone who couldn't accept me wholeheartedly, and if I hadn't felt the pain when we split up, I wouldn't have been prompted to go to therapy or find out what was going on in my inner world. I wouldn't have discovered that I had abandonment issues that were causing me to feel unworthy and undeserving of having an abundant life. I wouldn't have known I was disrespecting and dishonoring my life through self-sabotage. Sometimes, our greatest teachers are the people who touch us the deepest and make our hearts bleed, even though they have no intention to hurt us. Again, we get to choose our life's path by the thoughts we think and the emotions we feel, so choose wisely and honor yourself, especially when it comes to love.

Think about this scenario: Imagine you've come to the end of your exceptionally fulfilling life. What's going to be important to you at that moment? My guess is you'll be thinking about the people you loved and the people who loved you back. You're not going to care about your material possessions or even what you accomplished (although that may give you a huge degree of satisfaction).

Love is at the core of who we are and what we are here to share. It's an ever-present energy and our natural state of being. We're not here to hate others. We're loving creatures who sometimes get caught up in our pride and ego, but that's not our true essence. Let love flourish in your life in all forms. It's not an easy task at times, especially when we have different points of view, but just try to be more understanding and loving so love can flow back to you. It will make your life that much more beautiful.

Be kind, be patient, be compassionate, and above all, be your most authentic self. Let your essence be a blessing to everyone you encounter. As Anita Moorjani said, "The only purpose of life is to be our self, live our truth, and be the love that we are."

It's journaling time again. You're going to do a full-out, tell-it-like-it-is, pure and honest assessment of who you are and what you bring to the world merely by your presence in it. Please answer the following questions without judging yourself. Just be genuine and think of every amazing trait and quality you possess. Whether it's your smile, your sense of fun, your quiet demeanor that puts everyone at ease, your gregarious nature that keeps people laughing, your sense of organization, your heart, your skepticism, your questioning nature, or anything that makes you *you*, write it down. The point of this exercise is to start appreciating everything you bring to the table.

EXERCISE 1

Answer these questions to define what makes you, you.

1. What qualities and characteristics make you stand out in a crowd? What makes you unique?

2. What can you offer the world in your own way?

3. What do you most love about yourself?

EXERCISE 2

Repeat after me:

"I love myself exactly as I am, including all of my perceived imperfections."

Repeat again.

Repeat again with total conviction.

EXERCISE 3

Add this one question to your meditation practice.

"How can I use my special qualities to enhance the lives of others?"

Now that you're learning to embrace yourself fully and accepting that there's enough for everyone, it's time for some guidance on how to handle the roadblocks and challenges that may come your way.

CHAPTER 10

THE SHOW MUST GO ON!

*"Trust life, and it will teach you, in joy and
sorrow, all you need to know."*

— James Baldwin

As I was sitting at my desk writing this book in September 2020, the world was still in shut-down mode due to the pandemic. The invisible monster attacking humanity had taken its toll on a global level and it was no joke. People were dying as scientists and researchers worked tirelessly to find a cure. Life as we knew it ceased to exist. Businesses closed, people lost their jobs, and parents instantly had to become teachers. Restaurants, movie theaters, hair salons, non-essential businesses, and all of the places meant for us to have fun, relax, and socialize became non-existent. All of a sudden, we were living in a new and uncharted environment.

The entertainment business took a huge hit and performers who made their living playing in front of large crowds, like me, had been out of work since mid-March 2020. It was a very difficult time financially, mentally, and emotionally for many people, with no end in sight, with the exception of a possible treatment or vaccine on the horizon. So, we were all forced to begin thinking about reinventing ourselves and figuring out ways we could somehow still do what we love and make a living.

For entertainers and musicians, other than online concerts and shows, there were few places to perform. It seemed like this situation could become the wave of the future and our new normal could have ended up being like on *The Jetsons* cartoon from the 1960s where people did everything from the big screens in their living rooms. It was up to each individual to create new possibilities for themselves, and creativity abounded!

Zoom was no longer associated with an action verb but quickly became a household staple to communicate with friends and family. People adapted to working in their homes and children got to spend more time with their parents because of it. The entertainment world learned how to keep TV shows up and running, even if it meant gathering and editing video clips that people made in their homes. It was fun watching Stephen Colbert do his late-night show in his bathtub. As COVID-19 testing became more available, actors were able to get back on movie sets, sports teams were able to start playing, and businesses slowly started reopening.

We all had our eye on the end of the pandemic, but until then, we had to keep going as best we could. It gave us an opportunity to globally unite as a human family, and we all proved how resilient and adaptable we can be in the face of major challenges.

I couldn't help but look at all the good that was coming out of our global crisis. The air was getting cleaner because fewer cars were on the road, families were getting closer, and the things that truly mattered in life were taking the helm.

Simultaneously, with the unrest of the political climate, social upheaval, riots, and racial inequality being brought to the forefront, it was easy to get caught up in the negativity and fear. I chose to look for the positivity and noticed many people were becoming kinder and more compassionate. They were reaching out to help those in need, and whether through activism or one-on-one communications, their intent was to bring peace and unity to our world. By taking a higher perspective, I witnessed the true nature of who we are as loving, compassionate, and caring beings amid the craziness of the crisis.

It was truly a very scary and anxiety-ridden time, which is why I personally felt a need to rely on my spiritual practices. I trusted there was a bigger picture and did my best to remain peaceful and productive, attending to things that were lingering on my huge and ever-evolving to-do list. The shutdown gave me the gift of time to start attacking projects. I relied on the affirmation, *Life loves me, and I love life.* I knew deep down I could trust the process of life. However, I had one major challenge to deal with that *really* tested everything I knew to be true and everything I was writing about in this book.

COVID-19 hit me directly. I got sick.

Never in a million years did I think it would be possible to allow this virus into my body. I was too healthy, too positive, and too connected to the wholeness of who I was to entertain the thought of letting something serious invade my body. From the very beginning of the pandemic, every day I told my husband, "No pox for us!" (*Pox* being our code word for any kind of disease.) I visualized my healthy self and felt invincible!

We were fine for almost the entire year, and then in November 2020, during the second wave when COVID-19 numbers were rising rapidly, it happened. I got a call from one of my singer friends I'd seen a few days earlier. She said she had symptoms and had tested positive.

I still didn't believe I was going to get it. My husband and I got tested right away *just in case* we also had it and had exposed other people to it. We woke up at the crack of dawn and stood in a line outside an urgent care facility in the cold morning wind for five hours to get tested. They said we'd get the results in a couple of days.

The next day, I came down with flu-like symptoms that knocked me out of commission. Fever, chills, fatigue, and lower back pain kept me up at night and became my new normal as we waited five long days to get our test results. I didn't want to entertain the thought of having the virus, but during my lowest moments, I caved and allowed the thought into my mind. I wasn't fearful, but the thought of dying young made me realize how much I wanted to finish my book to get my message out there to help others.

I intuitively felt the illness was eventually going to pass, so I was gentle with myself and listened to what my body was telling me. If I was tired, I took a nap. In moments when I felt more alert, I mustered up the energy to sit in a chair and write. Yes, sitting in an upright position actually took strength.

I found that whenever I sat down to write, it instantly took the focus off my physical symptoms and made me feel better. I continually reminded myself to stay connected to spirit and trust that life had my back. I decided to let the chips fall where they may and not worry about it because I didn't need the extra stress. When the test results finally came back, both my husband and I tested negative. We both thought I must have gotten sick while waiting out in the cold for hours.

But then everything changed. My husband got very sick, and we both lost our sense of taste and smell. We knew we needed to get re-tested, and this time around, we were both positive. It was happening...we had gotten the *pox!* All the positive practices I had in place during that first week fell by the wayside as I became progressively weaker and more drained. I had no appetite, lost five pounds, and couldn't sleep. I was getting depressed and felt like the ever-cheerful, positive me had left the building. I was broken and initially afraid things were going to get worse.

Everything I needed to do mentally and spiritually, I wasn't doing. My soul knew better, so I put my earbuds in to listen to some healing meditations a couple of times right before I tried to sleep. They helped put my mind in a different state, but I realized I had some major lessons yet to learn, and I needed to practice what I preached. I needed to ride out the illness, be patient, and stay peaceful.

Writing has always been therapeutic for me, so I opened my journal and wrote a list of things I needed to concentrate on, which I intrinsically knew would make me feel better. Unconsciously, I ended up making a list that included many of the concepts I'm sharing in this book. Here is the advice I gave myself during the thick of my illness:

1.   What's my concern? My fear is that I'm going to get sicker and end up in a hospital on a respirator left to die alone. By thinking of the worst scenario, I'm causing myself more stress and anxiety. It's time to snap out of it and let my subconscious know this is just a temporary illness, and I'm on my way to healing. I know my Higher Self is stronger than my fears. My New Story: I am healing. I am getting stronger every day! The power within me knows exactly how to heal my body, and all I need to do is surrender to it, and let it do its thing.

2.   Trust the uncertainty and detach from the outcomes. I know life has my back, and I'm going to be fine no matter what happens.

3.   Stay connected spiritually. I'm here for a reason, and even if things do get worse, I'm comforted in my belief that we are eternal beings, and our souls don't die. We just move on to a new adventure.

4.   Keep meditating and stay mindful of thinking positive healing thoughts.

5.   Remain grateful—always. I'm still breathing and beyond grateful for that.

6.   Stay peaceful.

All these things became my way of staying calm, but during my physical decline, human fears sporadically reared their ugly head. It's especially easy to fall into fearful thoughts when you're dealing with health challenges. When your body is depleted, you're not thinking clearly, and that's when you need to delve inward. It's when you must acknowledge you're a walking miracle and the Divine power within you knows how to heal you. It's also the time to use your visualization skills to envision yourself as healthy and whole. With all of this in mind, during each of my writing sessions during the peak of my COVID-19 infection, I was *downloading* through the non-physical side of myself. I can compare this experience to walking on stage while sick as a dog and somehow getting through the performance. As they say, "The show must go on!"

After about a month of feeling physically awful, I felt my energy returning and made a pact to get back to my regular practices of doing yoga and listening to what my body was telling me when it came to exercising. I became more mindful of the food I ate and returned to my morning protein shakes instead of nibbling on saltines. I wanted to feel fully healthy again, so I tapped into my mind-body-spirit connection and felt grateful that I was one of the fortunate ones who didn't die alone in a hospital bed.

I continued feeling the side effects of the virus long after the initial phase; it was relentless. To add insult to injury, in April 2021, I got a call from a surgical center I'd been to a couple of days prior to get tests for my lingering health issues and was told a staff member who worked on me had tested positive for COVID-19! At that point, I had a choice. Would I freak out or calmly handle the news without worrying about it? I chose the latter.

Since singing is my career, I naturally began to get nervous that I would never sing again because the persistent health problem affected my voice, but then I reminded myself of my reason for still being here and of who I know myself to be, which is a Divine being of love, light, and joy. I knew that the *powers-that-be* were protecting me and life had my back, even though everything felt like it was falling apart. I felt more inspired to get my message out into the world because COVID-19 made it obvious how fragile life is and how we're all hanging on a string.

I made it a point to stay connected through meditation, and at my most fearful moments, I trusted that life was working in my favor no matter what happened. I also made use of affirmations. The most helpful affirmations for me in my state of anxiety were, *Every day in every way, I am getting stronger and healthier,* and Louise Hay's, *All is well in my world. Everything is working out for my highest good.* Instead of thinking about the possibilities of not being able to function as a singer, I surrendered my fears to the power that is greater than me and kept the faith that all would eventually be well, while reminding myself that everything happens with perfect timing. I made a deal with myself that if I couldn't get a handle on my physical issues and was no longer able to perform, I would accept it and acknowledge that life was pointing me in a new direction and toward a new dream.

Fortunately, after months of vocal therapy and medications, my voice started returning in mid-May 2021. I couldn't have been more grateful because that's when the world started opening up for entertainers. I finally felt the excitement in my bones of being able to perform again!

Fear can be debilitating. In the wisdom of Wayne Dyer, FEAR is just *false evidence appearing real.* We make up stories and accept them as truth when most of the time, they never come to pass. By doing this, we cause ourselves stress and anxiety, which work against us. When you find yourself facing your darkest fears, it's okay to recognize them, but don't let them overtake you. You're human, and it's inevitable something will happen to cause you to panic and think the worst. When this happens, acknowledge the fear, and give yourself a healthy dose of positive self-talk to turn it around. Ask yourself if the fear is based in truth or if you're making it up. Also, train yourself to stay in the present moment and not worry about what's going to happen down the road. No matter what challenges or unwelcome surprises life brings, do your best to dig deep into the wholeness of who you are to get through it.

My mother used to listen to singers from the 1950s. One of her favorites was Doris Day who sang "Que Sera Sera." Back then, I didn't recognize the life lesson contained in this song—simply accept that *what will be, will be.* We may never understand why things we see as bad happen to us or the world. Some people think we live in a random universe, but I wholeheartedly believe life happens on purpose and everything happens to help move us along on our journey.

What we can all agree on, philosophy aside, is that we get to choose how we handle life's tests. Every challenge has something to teach us, so we need to trust in the uncertainty and go with the flow of what's being presented to us. If we're mindful of what life is trying to teach us instead of focusing on why something is happening, we grow. We become stronger individuals and acquire a sense of power knowing we can handle whatever comes our way. On that note, life gave humanity yet one more challenge to deal with.

As the ball in Times Square dropped out of 2020 into 2021, humanity was filled with renewed hope and optimism for a better year since vaccines had been developed and were just starting to be distributed. But just a few days later, domestic terrorism hit the Capitol building, and we were once again raised to a new state of fear and unrest. On top of that, a new strain of the virus came into the picture that threatened to be more deadly than the first, which, at that time, had already killed nearly 400,000 people in the United States alone. My initial human instinct was along the lines of, *Really? Haven't we had enough to deal with already?*

I almost slipped into anxiety mode, but what quickly came to mind was a very useful tool used in Twelve-Step recovery programs—The Serenity Prayer. It's essentially the act of surrendering to a Higher Power and acknowledging you're not holding the reins to what's happening around you. If you're going through something you can't control, let it go and refer to these words: *God, grant me the serenity to accept the things I cannot change; courage to change the things I can; and wisdom to know the difference.*

Remember, your mission is to live a peaceful, happy, and fulfilling life, so the more you're able to let go of things that bother you that you can't do anything about, the less stress you'll be carrying around. Let's face it; war and peace will always be as evident on Earth as night and day because life contains contrasts to lead us to our Higher Selves. As individuals, we get to choose which side of the fence we want to be on—so choose wisely.

The challenges of 2020-2021 also reinforced the lesson that when faced with adversity, it's best to take your mind off what's happening to you and think about what you can do to help others. Creating this book took my mind off my own concerns and redirected my energies toward you and my other readers. I felt better by thinking about how you would be reading my book right now and how it would hopefully help you in some way. Remember in Chapter 2 when I asked you how you want to contribute to the world? Thinking about what you can do for others takes you out of *me* mode and into *how can I use my gifts to enhance the lives around me* mode? **Your life can be so much sweeter if you shine your light on the dimly lit path for another person.**

"You gain strength, courage, and confidence by every experience in which you really stop to look fear in the face. You must do the thing you cannot do."

— Eleanor Roosevelt

Each time you face a difficult situation, take a step back, breathe, and become aware of your thoughts and emotions. Are you fearful, sad, angry, anxious, or hurt? Are you focusing on the circumstance and why it happened? Are you facing a health challenge and thinking the most fearful thoughts about it? If so, it will benefit you to interrupt the fear-based thoughts, and change them right away. To do that, you have to start by accepting the situation. It is what it is, and the only thing you can do about it is figure out how you're going to deal with it.

Understand that you have the choice to hold on to fear or let it go. You get to choose thoughts that will keep you calm. As you now know, your life is based on the decisions you make, so change your thoughts and recite some affirmations that apply to your situation.

Guide your self-talk by telling yourself, "I'm stronger than I think I am. I'm going to be okay, no matter what happens. I've got this!" Keep in mind, also, that the invisible energy in you and around you is always accessible. You can surrender your concerns and worry over to it. It knows what's best for you, so you don't have to carry the heavy burden alone. You're never alone; you just think you are. You're always protected and guided by the ever-present energy inside you, but it's up to you to stay connected to it.

> *"Acknowledging the good that you already have in your life is the foundation for all abundance."*
>
> *— Eckhart Tolle*

Throughout 2020, an old adage kept popping up in my mind—*you don't know what you have until it's gone*. I was missing everything about my regular, beautiful life because I no longer had access to it. All sense of normalcy was gone, and only in retrospect, when you have lost everything, do you realize how much you cherish everything you had. Ziad K. Abdelnour, author of *Economic Warfare: Secrets of Wealth Creation in the Age of Welfare Politics*, said, "Learn to appreciate what you have before time makes you appreciate what you had." So, take a moment right now to savor all the goodness you have in your own life. Try to live your life focused on what's right in your world. You're alive, you're free to live the life you want, and you're loved. Above all, remember that every breath you take is a true gift. An attitude of gratitude will give you more to be grateful for and is yet another way to enrich your life.

> *"Worry often gives a small thing a big shadow."*
>
> — *Swedish Proverb*

"Sure, I'll concentrate on the good in my life, but what if something really bad happens?" you ask. I'm glad you did. To stay sane, you need to learn how to ride the waves as peacefully as possible. Many situations can disturb your peace and cause you concern about the future. As a human, you're very good at using your imagination to create stories based on your interpretation of the things going on around you. And you also know it's a personal decision whether you want to remain peaceful in the face of chaos or worry about everything that could possibly go wrong. Like an overly doting parent who is anxious about pretty much everything concerning their children, you're causing yourself unnecessary anxiety. You're fearful of future events that haven't even happened and convincing yourself of a false truth. It's not logical, and yet so many people continue to do this.

I come from a family of worriers—that's right, *worriers*, not *warriors*. Both my mother and grandmother taught me to worry about everything. They obviously didn't know what I know now. Worry is simply the act of creating a story about something that hasn't happened yet, and more than likely, never will. Why do that to yourself? It seems logical to opt for peace, but the tendency for most people is to worry.

So how do you stop the habit of worrying? Mindfulness. Just be aware of your thoughts, and ask yourself if the story you've created is true. If it's not, relax and let it go. Change your thought to focus on reality, not on what can go wrong. Stay in the moment, which is where truth is, and rely on your faith that life is on your side. When you stay present in your *now*, you're not worrying about what's going to happen in the future or thinking about what happened in the past or trying to analyze everything. You're just present, right here, right now, soaking it all in and experiencing it fully. Most people live their lives more in the past and the future than in the moment. Save yourself the misery, and live out your life as each moment presents itself. Spiritual leader Father Richard Rhor eloquently said, "All stress comes from not accepting what's happening in the present moment. If you accept your *what-is*, you can find contentment."

The next time you are concerned and worry starts to set in, face it head on. Instead of ruminating about it, physically flick it away with your fingers and tell it, *no thank you*! Once you begin changing your thoughts and accepting that life is going to unfold the way it's supposed to, you'll be rid of negative energy and start clearing the way for all of the goodness of life.

Learn to go with the flow and accept that life brings you what you need. Learn to accept and face challenges knowing they're meant to help you learn and grow. Everything that comes your way is a gift because whether you interpret it as good or bad, it's there for a reason. As the great philosopher Socrates said, "The only thing I know is that I know nothing, and I am not quite sure that I know that." You're never going to know the reasons things happen the way they do, so accept them as they come. Do whatever you can to help yourself out of situations, but do it from a sense of calmness, not anxiety.

"Don't try to steer the river."

— Deepak Chopra

Let's talk about another practice for finding your peace. It can be summed up in three words—detach from outcomes.

I grew up near a beach and used to love making sandcastles. With my tiny shovel and pail, I would pick the perfect spot far enough away from the flowing movement of the ocean tides so the water couldn't wash it away. I'd also dig a hole right next to my *palace-to-be* to stand in if the sand got too hot. I'd make sure it was deep enough so I could feel the water come in under my toes. Why am I bringing this up? Well, within that timeframe of creating my masterpiece by throwing buckets of sand on top of each other and sculpting them to my liking, I was totally in the moment and enjoying every second of it. It made me feel happy and alive.

Eventually, the tide caught up to my castle and washed it away. I had no pictures of what I had just spent time putting together, but the experience of joy was lasting enough to make me want to do it over and over again. I didn't know it then, but I realized later that this is the perfect way to live our lives. Do what you love, stay fully in the moment, experience the joy, and detach from the outcome. And like the ocean itself, stay in the flow and ride the tide peacefully in and out.

"Embrace the uncertainty. Enjoy the beauty of becoming. When nothing is certain, anything is possible."

— Mandy Hale

Remember Jack Canfield's equation, E + R = O? I believe there's another element to this equation. Although we have control over our responses and can alter them by the way we think, we don't actually have control over outcomes. Life has the final say. It will give us what we need but not necessarily what we had in mind. It may lead us somewhere we never expected to be and leave us pleasantly surprised. Successful people know how to handle disappointment and keep moving forward, but those who resist what life is giving them won't get positive results. They're working against the tide of life instead of flowing with it. I know it's really cliché to say, but it's true that when one door closes, another *will* open.

We've talked about the act of surrendering when it comes to situations we can't change and accepting that life knows what it's doing. I sometimes refer to God as *Life* because I know that this magical energy is in charge of what's going on. With free will, we get to create our lives by our responses to what is unfolding around us. However, the final outcome is never up to us. Let go of your need to control outcomes, and let life guide you toward your highest potential. ***The Universe knows how to get you where you want and need to be and will do so in its own perfect timing.***

All you need to do is figure out what it is you truly want, why you want it, and truly believe you're going to get it. Napoleon Hill said, "You are the master of your destiny. You can influence, direct, and control your own environment. You can make your life what you want it to be."

We absolutely have control over what's going on inside of us. Our outside environment reflects our thoughts, emotions, and actions. However, we need to stay focused on our vision even if our circumstances aren't quite in line with our hopes. We need to trust the timing and roll with whatever comes our way while keeping the faith that we *will* get there. If you don't get the job you really, really wanted, instead of feeling dejected, trust that opportunities will be coming your way and they will be the right fit for you. In the words of Pastor Joel Osteen, "Setbacks are usually set-ups for something greater to come to you."

Not only is it beneficial to trust in the uncertainty of life, but it's best to embrace it fully because you don't know what magic lies beyond. The Universe dreams bigger dreams than you could ever imagine. Even if you don't believe in God, how do you feel knowing life could be giving you opportunities you never thought of? This is a strong possibility if your vision for life is clear. As we discussed in the chapter on visualizations, if you feel the excitement as if it's already happening, and if you're focused and taking action toward where you want to be, everything that is meant for you will come to you. You need to develop 100 percent certainty that you can trust life and know without a doubt that it's always working on your behalf. It may not appear that way when things are going wrong or you're faced with major challenges, but again, everything happens *for* you and not *to* you. Choose to accept whatever comes your way and lean into the inner knowledge that you are safe.

> *"We must have a pie. Stress cannot exist in the presence of a pie."*
>
> *— David Mamet*

Even though we're spiritual beings at the core, we're still human and still prone to getting stressed out. If you are friends with me on

Facebook, you might remember I posted a question asking everyone how they handled stress. The answers included meditation, exercise, yoga, singing, listening to music, hot baths, dancing, walking in nature, talking to friends, calling a therapist, praying, binge-watching TV shows, and the not-so-self-serving responses of binge-eating, drinking, and slamming things against a wall. Whatever gets you through stressful moments and brings you peace will work, but make sure you don't linger in the stress zone or hurt anyone in the process.

In the past, I used to relieve stress by working out or punching a *Slam Man*. These days, my stress is usually caused by my enormous self-inflicted to-do lists. When I'm overwhelmed, I know I can close my eyes, take a few deep breaths, reconnect to my Higher Self, and reboot to peace and calm. I use the words, *I surrender. I let go. I allow and I accept.* This process gets me out of my head and back to feeling centered. I lean on my faith that all's well no matter what seems to be falling apart in my outside world.

By "letting go and letting God," you're instantly giving your concerns over to your Higher Self, which always dwells in a space of peace. Whatever works to get you into a happier headspace is fine, but meditation is the quickest way to reset, even if it's just for a few minutes. ***When you're in the midst of challenges, learn how to take a time-out to tune-in.*** By creating this habit for yourself, you'll become less reactive and better equipped to handle whatever challenges come your way.

Pop quiz! What can you do to help yourself if life feels out of control?

    A) Meditate and recite some affirmations

    B) Write in your journal to clear your head

C) Choose a new story

D) Take a few deep breaths to reset your thoughts and emotions

E) All of the above

I have no doubt you picked the right answer. You can use any or all of the above techniques to handle overwhelming, stressful situations. Pick the tools above that work for you and always choose peace as your goal. Being constantly nervous, tense, or frazzled doesn't serve you or your higher purpose. Try always to choose peace, regardless of your external circumstances. If you need to work off your stress doing something physical, take a walk, visit the gym, or do a quick workout at home just to get your endorphins flowing. The more you incorporate new habits for dealing with mental and emotional burdens, the less you'll feel the effects in your body. You'll know how to deal with challenging situations more efficiently and be able to process things more easily when they come up again.

To help you get through a crisis, bring to mind the Yiddish phrase, "Gam Zeh Ya'avor" which translates to "This too shall pass," and know that everything is in constant flux. You'll get through your difficult moments and move on. Need I remind you one more time that you're stronger than you think you are? You have power within that is more than your circumstances or conditions. You can face anything that comes your way once you start trusting that life is on your side.

"People rarely succeed unless they have fun in what they are doing."

— Dale Carnegie

Let's switch gears right now. If someone asked if you were enjoying your life, what would you say? Could you respond with a smile and say you feel blessed to be doing what you love and getting paid for it? If not, it's time to become more mindful of how your time here on Earth is passing and how much you deserve to live out your dreams. Think about how you would feel if everything you truly desired was yours. Your life would be fulfilling and *fun*!

Having a balance between work and play is essential to happiness, but what if you were to merge work and play so they totally aligned with what your soul wants you to do? I can tell you from experience that it's an amazing feeling. You don't need to struggle through your days and settle for less than you deserve. You get to choose what makes you feel happy and totally alive. There's that word *choose* again. I think by now you understand that only you can make changes in your life, and you do this by the choices you make. Choose wisely and follow your joy.

As you know, life isn't always rosy; it can be a complex web of obligations, to-do lists, and tests of your patience. Handling the many roles you play at home and work can sometimes feel daunting and very draining. To offset the tension, take time out of your day to relax and enjoy simple moments. Think back to when you were a kid with no responsibilities. How did you spend your time? Were you out playing with your friends or pets? Whether it involved sports, boardgames, bike riding, playing an instrument, reading, or watching a movie, you were doing something fun—something you loved to do. The yin-yang balance is crucial to avoiding burnout, so make the time to take care of yourself. A balanced life is a happy life.

In the 1960s, Simon and Garfunkel captured the feeling of moving too fast in "The 59th Street Bridge Song (Feelin' Groovy)," which alluded to slowing down because we're moving too fast. I encourage you to slow down to avoid burnout. Take time out of your busyness to reboot and refresh yourself, even if it's only for a few minutes. Your life will flow much more smoothly if you allow yourself small breaks.

Also back in the 1960s, Indian mystic Meher Baba often used the expression, "Don't worry, be happy." It was printed on inspirational cards and posters throughout the decade. Bobby McFerrin later used the catchphrase in his song of the same name—I dare you not to sing it right now. It's such a simple little ditty, yet it's packed with so much wisdom.

Your exercises for this chapter have to do with how you're facing challenges daily. These exercises are recommended for when you encounter stress, fear, anxiety, or feel overwhelmed.

EXERCISE 1

During your day, become mindful of your thoughts. If something comes up that causes you anxiety or fear, take out your journal and write down what's bothering you and the fear behind your concerns. Is this a fearful thought about what might happen (aka worry), or is it something you need to act on? Is it something you can control? If it's pure worry and a fear-based story you're making up, rewrite it in your mind, and then write it down. Re-read your new story a few times until you feel calmer.

EXERCISE 2

If you feel yourself becoming overwhelmed, reset your body and mind. Take some deep breaths and/or take a few minutes to sit in stillness. Silently repeat these words: "I surrender. I let go. I go with the flow."

EXERCISE 3

Schedule some downtime in your day to relax, have fun, and play! If you're having a hard day, it's even more important to give yourself a tension break and get your mind off whatever's troubling you. Let your mind, body, and spirit be free from any cares or concerns. Even if it's only for a few minutes, this is your time to let go, be carefree, frolic *in joy*, and savor the moment.

In the next chapter, we're going to stay on the topic of life's uncertainty but take a more in-depth look at how to handle roadblocks and make empowering decisions.

CHAPTER 11

TRUST YOUR INNER GUIDE

*"When life is falling apart, things could
actually be falling together."*

— Neale Donald Walsch

In the last chapter, you learned to trust life and have faith that you can handle whatever comes your way. We're going to take this a step further to discuss what happens when you hit roadblocks because they either teach you something or move you in a different direction. The journey to happiness and success isn't always a smooth ride. We all encounter bumps, potholes, and muddy puddles that dirty our path.

It's important to give yourself an internal power wash when you're feeling frustrated, upset, disappointed, angry, and all of the negative emotions that, as humans, we can't help but feel. Take the time to let your body experience and process these emotions, but after allowing yourself to wallow in that space, give yourself a spiritual cleansing by turning inward. Remember, your peace lies within. Only you can choose to move toward calmness and acceptance, especially about situations you can't control.

You can't help feeling the suckiness of your challenges as you're going through them, but they're actually there for your own good. It's in your best interest to trust that. Life lessons lie within the murkiness of each setback or disappointment. Usually, this is just life giving you the opportunity to self-assess and grow. You can't control what happens around you, but you can control what happens within you. My advice is always to choose peace. I know it's not easy, and some situations are harder than others to endure, but let peace be your goal. And remember, you always have a powerful presence within to help you through the messy bits.

I had never heard of the concept of choosing peace until I was in my forties. Being in show business, I certainly wish I had known about that option sooner. I've faced more than my share of rejection and can attest to the fact that it can tear your insides out if you let it. Up until I knew what I know now, I let it get to me. At each audition, I'd put my heart and soul into the performance only to get, "Thank you for coming" or "We'll be in touch" or if I was lucky, "We'd like you to come to a callback." In any profession, searching for work is a job in itself, and most people in all walks of life understand that rejection is just part of the process. Doesn't it make sense simply to move on instead of driving yourself crazy? Give yourself time to feel the disappointment, but choose not to dwell in that state because it doesn't serve you. Choose peace.

In 2008, one of my favorite singer-girlfriends, Nancy Bender, and I headed down to Nashville to audition for a new show on CMT (Country Music Television) called *Can You Duet*. Nancy was no stranger to TV talent shows. She had already been a finalist on Ed

McMahon's *Star Search*, but I had never experienced this kind of competition before.

We got in line at 5 a.m. and waited in the freezing cold to get our chance to sing. We had rehearsed Dusty Springfield's "Son of a Preacher Man" and were ready to give it our best shot.

Hours passed by before we finally got our chance. We nailed the first audition and were asked to stick around for round two. After a short wait in a holding area with other competitors who had been asked to stay, our names were called and we were brought into a room to sing in front of new judges. This time, a camera was set up to film our audition. We were also interviewed to get a sense of our personalities and who we were. They seemed interested, and we left feeling hopeful and on a complete high. But we never heard from them. Despite the long wait and the disappointing outcome, it was a fun and exhilarating day, so I wanted more of the reality competition world.

In 2011, another new TV talent show came along called *The X-Factor*. I was beyond excited to audition since I was too old to be considered for *American Idol* where the cut-off age was twenty-eight. I told all my singer friends about the show and couldn't have been more hyped up to go for it.

When they announced the audition details, my bubble burst. The auditions were being held in five different cities around the country, and in each instance, the timing made it impossible for me. I had a day job that was very flexible around my singing schedule except for a two-week period when they needed me to be there. As life would have it, the auditions were during that two-week period. I was devastated. But once the sting of disappointment went away, I realized it was out of my control, and I accepted that it wasn't meant to be.

Later that year, a new show premiered called *The Voice*. I auditioned three times but never got a callback. Many of my mega-talented singer friends also auditioned without getting on the show. My jaw dropped when I heard they either didn't make it past the second callback or didn't get asked to stay past the first round. The world is full of incredibly talented people, but with reality competitions, it's hard to know what they're looking for.

The third time I auditioned for *The Voice*, I just wasn't feeling the excitement I had felt during my Nashville trip. I realized I was already making a living as a singer and didn't have a strong desire to be a solo artist because I loved working with groups and bands. I also recognized that I feed off the energy of my fellow musicians and love singing harmony, so it was an epiphany of sorts that I no longer needed to entertain the thought of flying solo on reality TV.

I also learned both success and failure are essential tools for self-discovery. No experiences are ever wasted since they are the pathway to growth. Think about it. You learn to walk by falling down and getting right back up. If you approach failure with this mindset, it will be easier to manage the disappointments and use them to your benefit. As Sonia Ricotti, author of *Unsinkable*, said, "Failure is another word for feedback." And Thomas Edison affirmed, "I have not failed. I have just found 10,000 ways that will not work."

Keep in mind that when you make mistakes, there's no need to beat yourself up over it. Consider it merely part of your growth. You learn, and the next time, you do better. Oprah Winfrey describes our world as *Earth School*. Opportunities are continuously given to us to challenge us, to increase our knowledge, to expand and grow. It's all a process on the journey to becoming our best selves.

With all my disappointments and perceived failures, I learned a few things. When you grow from the lessons you've learned, you've added another ring to your ever-growing tree of wisdom. In my case, being in show biz, I realized it was best not to take things personally. This principle applies to every profession, especially during job interviews. Rejection can make you doubt yourself, but it doesn't have to be that way. Instead of telling yourself you aren't good enough or worthy of getting the job, recognize that the people interviewing you are looking for something specific. In their eyes, you may be over-qualified, under-qualified, too young, too old, too quiet, too loud…you name it. Whoever they end up hiring will be someone who resonates with them, and unfortunately, you have no say in the matter. Accept it and move on.

Choose to keep your peace instead of being frustrated and let down. Choose to let go of that one disappointing rejection that wasn't meant for you. Give yourself a pep talk and recite some affirmations confirming how talented and valuable you are. In other words, show yourself some self-love when you need it the most.

Winston Churchill said, "Success consists of going from failure to failure without loss of enthusiasm." Learn from your mistakes and know that failing is the greatest tool for helping you grow because it makes you aware of what you can do better next time.

It's also important to acknowledge your small successes along the way as they eventually lead to bigger ones. Life will always give you opportunities to become better at what you need to learn the most.

My dear friend Rick, whom I've known since first grade, is the *make lemons into lemonade* type. His dream in high school was to be a professional baseball player, but due to physical issues and life circumstances, he wasn't able to pursue his heart's desire. Naturally, the initial realization that he couldn't get what he really wanted was a hard hit, but he moved on to doing something else he enjoyed. In other words, he allowed himself to feel the emotional weight of the letdown, but then, in typical Rick fashion, got back on his feet and made some lemonade. He instinctively made the choice to make the best of his circumstances. You can too. Remember, you get to choose your thoughts, which then lead to your actions.

A prime example of someone who picked herself up after being shot down is powerhouse singer Marisa Corvo. I met Marisa in 2011 when we sang together in her father's wedding band. I was pleasantly surprised to find that she had made it onto the 2020 season of *The Voice*.

At the time, she was in her mid-twenties and felt defeated because a publishing deal for her original music had fallen through. Additionally, she had auditioned twelve times for *American Idol* but was turned down each time. She was burnt out, ready to hang it up, and told me she wanted a simple life. That all changed in 2012 when her father convinced her to audition one more time. She decided to go for it and, this time, made it onto the show! She made it all the way through to the Las Vegas rounds right before the live shows aired. This experience sparked her desire to continue her career and she took action to make it happen. She moved to California, started doing solo gigs, had chance encounters with music celebrities, and was personally invited by acclaimed songwriter Diane Warren to premiere one of her songs.

Marisa's tenacity, drive, and determination to be her best is an inspiration to each of us to follow our heart's desires. Even when she got cut from *The Voice* by her coach Kelly Clarkson to the shock of millions, Marisa admitted that although she was disappointed, she had other opportunities to promote her own music coming her way. She continued to inspire others by the grace with which she handled the rejection and how she acknowledged the positives that came from that experience.

"Everyone is figuring it out as they go. Don't let someone else tell you how it is supposed to be, just because they say they know better. Be brave enough to make your own messes."

— Sama Akbar

Face it; you're going to make mistakes because you're human. It's okay. Just keep picking yourself up and moving forward toward where you want to be. One of the easiest ways to get to your destination is to rely on your internal GPS. Inside each of us, we have an innate guide. We're born with it, but if we don't know it's there, we're not able to rely on it.

If you use Waze and Google Maps when you're driving, you know all you have to do is program where you want to go, and the GPS knows the quickest way to get you there. You normally don't question it. You simply follow the directions while staying in the lanes it advises you to be in. Similarly, we can do this with our lives. Some call it intuition, some call it instinct, and Oprah Winfrey calls it our *emotional GPS*. Whatever the label, it's there to guide us along the way. It's an inner knowing that doesn't come from our rational mind. All we need to do is remain aware of it and listen to what it's telling us.

You might ask, "But how do I differentiate my inner GPS voice from all of the other voices floating around in my head?" Just know that your inner voice is always calm and never flustered. It's non-judgmental and will give you signals and suggestions. You'll intuitively feel like you're being guided. Gandhi said, "The voice for truth speaks to every person on the planet, every single day, and that voice is as loud as our willingness to listen." Your inner intelligence knows exactly what you need to do, so tap into it as much as you can. If you need help with something, you can ask specific, targeted questions like you do with search engines. For instance, ask yourself, "What can I do today that will move me toward my dreams?" and then listen for the answers. Your intuition knows all, and the more you tune into it, the faster you'll get to point B.

Always trust your gut instincts because your intellect is only part of the decision-making process. If you come across a situation where you're indecisive and your thoughts are taking you in circles, the best thing to do is check in with your heart to observe your emotions and what they're telling you. Pay attention to the physical sensations in your body, which are signs to guide you. If your stomach is churning or you're feeling tension in your chest, or tightness wherever your body holds stress, it's a signal that something's not right and you need to avoid making any quick decisions. If something feels wrong, it is. If it feels right, it is.

For the ultimate results when making decisions, surrender the issue to your Higher Wisdom by closing your eyes, taking a few deep breaths, and tuning into your inner space. Ask yourself how to handle the situation, and then sit in silence and observe what comes to you. Simply let go and listen to what your inner voice tells you. This is your God-self speaking to you, and it knows what's best. As Wayne Dyer puts it, "If prayer is you talking to God, then your intuition is God talking to you." All the answers are within you. All you need to do is tune inward to get them. I wish I had known this in my younger years because I came across many circumstances that didn't feel right, and I did it anyway, only to feel even worse.

I was taunted and left feeling far less than peaceful because I dwelled in disempowering states. I remained stuck in fear, doubt, and disappointment, but by the mere act of becoming more aware of what felt right to me at the core and trusting my instincts, I was able to transform to a new level of feeling empowered and completely authentic. Whenever people give me advice now, I've learned to adopt only those suggestions that resonate within. Everyone has an opinion, but it is your life to live the way you want. If you listen to your inner wisdom at all times, your life will flow along gracefully.

Part of surrendering is being a clear channel to accept the direction of your internal guide. If you're living in shame or guilt or having a hard time letting go of resentment, let's take a moment to talk about forgiveness. To live a joyful life, you'll need to let go of the negativity you carry around with you.

"Forgiveness doesn't excuse past behavior that caused you pain; forgiveness prevents your past pain from destroying your future."

— *Tiffani Patlan*

I've done stupid things I could either beat myself up over for a lifetime or choose to forgive myself for not knowing any better. I eventually chose the latter because the first approach wasn't working for me. One thing that used to haunt me was a decision I made while on vacation with my mother. We used to take trips together every now and then, and one of her dreams was to go to Disney World. The day had finally come, and we hopped on a plane to Orlando on our way to a fun adventure together. It was raining when we arrived, so we decided to hold off on going to the theme parks until the next day when the sun was supposed to be shining and spent the rest of our day visiting relatives.

The next morning at breakfast, I noticed a classified ad in the local newspaper looking for a singer for a musical production. I asked my mother if it would be okay if we made a pitstop before heading to the parks, and she said, "Of course." So, we drove over to the audition.

I ended up getting the job and asked when I needed to start. They said, "Now!" They told me I would have to begin immediately because the show was only two weeks away, and I had a lot of material to learn. I was torn, but at that time, I had just finished the cruise ship gig and was looking for opportunities to perform again. My mother left it up to me, saying she'd be disappointed if I couldn't stay with her, but that she'd understand if I chose to take the job.

I decided to take the gig but felt horrible afterwards. Fast forward years later, my mother was diagnosed with a lymphoma on her optic nerve, went through a horrible two-year period of cancer treatments, and then passed away. We never made it to Disney World. To this day, the guilt pops up, and I have to consciously remember that if I had been more awakened back then, I would have made a healthier decision. It took me years to forgive myself for that incident.

In retrospect, I realize my decision to leave her was very selfish. I know my mother always wanted the best for me and probably accepted that I was determined to keep building my career, but at the same time, I didn't consider how upset she must have been in that moment. I never even asked her what she ended up doing after I left. It was all about me, and I regret that. I was grasping at straws and not trusting that something better would come along. It weighed on me for a very long time, but then I learned the power of forgiveness.

> "To forgive is to set a prisoner free and discover
> that the prisoner was you."
>
> — Lewis B. Smedes

Forgiving yourself for things you've done or said because you didn't know any better at the time is important to keeping your peace. When you don't forgive yourself, you carry around all the negative emotions from the particular incidents. Self-forgiveness is necessary to release yourself from the chains of guilt and shame. These lower levels of energy only serve to disempower you and keep you from evolving into the peaceful, joyful life you seek. Understand that you've grown and now operate from a different mindset and heart space. What's done is done, and there's no need to keep reliving the past. View the past as a gateway that led you to where you are now and helped you grow into the person you are today.

Self-forgiveness is a way to release old wounds. The more compassionate and understanding you are with yourself, the more you become an open vessel for your bright future. Eventually, the new and improved version of *you* is going to be comforting your younger self whenever old thoughts enter your mind. You'll feel more self-assured because you've recognized you'll do better next time. The right responses and decisions were always available to you, but they were clouded by past pain. What's truly important is your *now*, so release the old pain, forgive yourself, and start creating the awesome life you deserve.

"Forgive them, for they know not what they do."

— Luke 23:34

Sometimes people say or do things that cause us to feel angry, upset, hurt, shamed, disappointed, or downright frustrated. The worst thing to do is blame the person who said or did this to you.

I can hear your reaction loud and clear. "What? Are you kidding? Do you know what that SOB did to me? Are you nuts?"

Okay, let me explain why I'm saying this. By placing blame, you allow others to have power over you and let them determine your actions. You are the owner of your thoughts, so you can choose how you want to respond to each situation. No one can *make you* feel bad unless you choose to allow yourself to feel that way.

As humans with sensitive egos, it's sometimes easier said than done, but if you want to live a happy life, you must choose peaceful thoughts and let things slide. Anger will only keep you in a disempowered vibrational state, and that's not what you want. You are the only one with power over your life and how you respond to circumstances.

Yes, you, and you alone, determine how you're going to process insults and hurtful remarks. It's okay to respectfully stand up for yourself and tell the other person they're entitled to their opinion, but don't let their thoughtless or hurtful words linger inside of you. If you choose to continue arguing, the other person is just going to keep attacking you. Let them spread their venom elsewhere on someone who will accept the bite.

When you hold onto a grudge, you're only hurting yourself, so let it go and move on. "I can forgive, but I can't forget," you say? Well, if you keep reminding yourself about the experience that made your emotions boil, you're going to keep making yourself feel angry and hurt. Don't do this to yourself. You're bigger than that one experience. You have a beautiful life to lead, and nothing can get in your way but you.

Mahatma Gandhi said, "The weak can never forgive. Forgiveness is the attribute of the strong." And the Buddha said, "Holding onto anger is like grasping a hot coal with the intent of throwing it at someone else; you are the one who gets burned."

On that note, try to live from a state of compassion and love. The person who did you harm most likely has their own set of issues to deal with and may not be as thoughtfully awake as you are. You may not know their whole story, and chances are, they are as broken inside as you were in the past.

Let's put the concept of forgiveness into practice with the following exercises.

EXERCISE 1: FORGIVE OTHERS

Step 1:

In your journal, write down anything that's bothering you, either a recent event or something from the past that you still carry on your shoulders.

Step 2:

When you've written everything you needed to get out of your system, acknowledge and write down the emotions that came up while you were writing. Start with the words, "I felt...."

Step 3:

Recognize how these feelings keep you in a low vibrational state. Instead of stewing in these negative emotions, forgive the other person and release the thoughts of the incident from your mind. Know that by doing this, you're helping yourself move in a new and happier direction. Once you've reframed the incidents in your mind, you may still remember them, but you won't get wrapped up in them. You will have accepted that you didn't have control over whatever another said or did, and you have the choice to respond with peace. They can no longer hurt you if you don't allow them to. Choose to let your grudges go and entertain only uplifting and positive thoughts. And remember, you're doing this for yourself!

Step 4:

Your last action step is to write down the name of the person or persons who harmed you, and tell them you forgive them for how they hurt you. Forgive them, and if you can find it in your heart, wish them well. In other words, take the high road because it always leads to a higher state of being.

EXERCISE 2: FORGIVE YOURSELF

Write an apology letter to yourself for any crappy things you've done that still bother or disturb you. Include all the particulars of what you did along with why you did it. Think back to how things would have been different if you had known better at the time. If you've harmed anyone or said anything hurtful, you may want to make amends with them to clear the air if the relationship is important to you. Hopefully, you now know that you can change your response to confrontations and choose to live in peace.

Next up, we'll talk about aligning with your dream and take a more in-depth look at how to deal with fear and self-doubt. But first, we'll look at deciding whether to stay or leave a job that's sucking the life out of you.

CHAPTER 12

STAY TRUE TO YOURSELF

"To thine own self be true."

— *Act 1, Scene 3, Shakespeare's* Hamlet

Life shouldn't be about working for a paycheck. We all deserve so much more than that. As you discovered in prior chapters, it's important to stay authentically true to who you are and why you're here. It's very easy to lose sight of your bigger picture when you feel stuck in an unfulfilling day job, so let's talk about this aspect of your life.

Are you happy at your job? If not, what's missing? Do you wake up excited to go to work? Does your job bring you joy and make you feel alive? If not, read on.

I had someone tell me years ago to get a *real* job, and then it happened again when I went to a temp agency to get part-time, supplemental work. The very polite woman interviewing me asked what I was good at, and when I told her I was a professional singer, she said, "Well, you can't make a living doing that. Wouldn't it be wise to find something else to do to bring in a steady income?"

At first, I was taken aback that my profession was being judged as not a *real* one. But then I found that these comments gave me more fuel to keep doing what I love because it's what made me happy. Thus, the reason for this book. It's important to live from your truth to make your life extraordinary. This is *your* life to create, and you choose how to play it out. In the words of Wayne Dyer, "What other people think of you is none of your business." Similarly, Apple co-founder Steve Jobs said, "Don't let the noise of others' opinions drown your own inner voice. And most important, have the courage to follow your heart and intuition. They somehow already know what you truly want to become."

As an entertainer, I'm no stranger to the concept of having to do something other than what you love to pay the bills. Unlike a nine-to-five job, there's no consistency in the work life of an actor, singer, or dancer. You do a show, the show ends, and then you audition for another one. During those off times, you still need to pay the rent.

When I moved to New York City, I had no money other than what I had made on the cruise ship, so I needed to find work right away. Since I already had waitressing experience from working my way through college, I immediately took on a waitressing job and found a place to live, which ended up being a small, closet-sized room furnished with a twin bed, a dresser, and a shared kitchen and bathroom with the other tenants. I hated it, but it was my own space, and I was in the heart of New York City where I wanted to be.

I chose waitressing not only to pay the rent but to get a decent meal. I was literally living hand-to-mouth. I didn't know anyone in the city, so I called upon my own strength to get me through whatever challenges I met. I felt alone but still persevered on my quest to become successful doing what I loved. It wasn't easy, and at first, I was purging my anxieties with Twinkies and cupcakes while my clothes started getting tighter and tighter.

Every day, I checked the show business trade papers to see what auditions were being held. If something sounded appealing to me, I went and gave it my best shot. I ended up doing the three-month stint in Florida at a dinner theater, came back to New York City afterwards, and then landed a gig singing in a show band. Show bands became my comfort zone and learning ground for a couple of years. For the first time, I went on tour and was given my own hotel room. Having my own luxurious space was heaven! Just like the cruise gig, I was being paid to sing and dance *and* was given a place to stay with large closets and maid service.

When the band parted ways, I went back to waitressing and doing temp jobs until my next gig came along. This wandering from job to job became my normal, and I realized it was the way show biz operated. My skills got stronger just by singing six nights a week, but I wasn't nearly where I wanted to be, and I was still poor and living paycheck-to-paycheck.

Fortunately, things turned around when I auditioned for a club date agency that hired vocalists to sing for corporate parties and weddings. The money for one gig was quadruple what I was getting paid from the show band, so I worked tirelessly to learn new songs because my repertoire had to include all different styles of music. It was a fertile time of growth, and I stayed in that world for more than thirty years while pursuing different musical projects along the way. Although the money was great, one of my temporary day jobs wanted to hire me on seasonally during the winters, which was perfect because not many singing jobs were to be had at that time of year. I held onto that job for the flexibility and additional income, but I never lost sight of my dreams. I trusted that life would take me where it wanted me to be.

In a world where money matters, many people gravitate toward finding a job with benefits that will provide a steady paycheck. However, in the process, they lose sight of themselves and their true purpose. They get stuck in a job that leaves them exhausted and unfulfilled with no time to figure out what they're really put on Earth to do. Be very clear about why you are here, and always keep your Higher Vision in mind when you're making decisions. As a refresher, refer back to your answers from Chapter 2 if you haven't looked at them for a while. Have you remained true to yourself?

There's a life-force inside you looking to express itself through your unique gifts and abilities. It's your reason for being here, and it's up to you to use what you were given at birth to the fullest extent. You might unconsciously block your purpose by getting stuck in an unfulfilling day job.

I pose to you this one question:

Should you quit your day job?

I can hear the sighs and rebuttals already. "I want to quit my day job, but I have a family to feed and a mortgage to pay," or "I know I'm not fulfilled, but I'm making a good living and have financial security."

Are you really making a good living, though? How are you defining the word *good*? Does your job have anything to do with your true desires and passions? Are you using the innate natural abilities you were born with? Do you head to work every day excited and happy to be doing what you're doing? Is your work your play? If you answered "no" to these questions, then you're simply existing to pay the bills and not thriving. You deserve better than that!

When I graduated from college, I tried out a number of different *real* jobs. Aside from waitressing, I was an administrative assistant at a local United Way, worked in a podiatrist's office as a receptionist, was a chiropractic assistant, did several office temp jobs, and trained one day as an ophthalmologist's assistant, which was way beyond me. None of them thrilled me the way performing does, and I intrinsically knew I had to pursue my passions to be happy. I acted upon my instincts because it was a burning desire, and I encourage you to do the same.

I'm not suggesting you quit your job or that you never work a day job to supplement the income from what you really love to do. Depending on your life and financial circumstances, it's best to do what feels right for you. If you don't have sufficient funds to take care of yourself or your family, then making an immediate move would be a really bad idea. I'm simply suggesting that you don't get stuck forever in the nine-to-five grind of doing something you dislike or are doing just for a paycheck because that will be a wasted and unfulfilling life. In the book, *Theodore Roosevelt: An Autobiography*, Roosevelt states, "Do what you can, with what you've got, where you are."

If you're an artist of any kind, it's difficult pulling in a steady stream of income unless you're well known, so my advice is to stick to part-time jobs that give you the flexibility to seek out your path to success. For business-minded individuals with corporate jobs who aren't happy, in your spare time, research jobs better suited to you. Take baby steps to make the transition. Dolly Parton wisely said, "Don't get so busy making a living that you forget to make a life."

Take a moment right now to visualize yourself at ninety. Will you look back on your life with a smile because you lived fully and became the best version of yourself you could possibly be by staying true to who you knew you were? Or will you look back with regret at the things you wish you would have done but you never got around to doing because you were too busy to step out of your comfort zone? Every decision you make in the present will influence the rest of your life, so choose wisely, my friend. This is your life, and you deserve to be happy and fulfilled!

Now, if you are already financially secure and considering going full out with a major career change, I encourage you to make it happen. Take the risk, learn what you need to know, take action, and go for it. If you follow your heart and do what lights you up, you will never regret it.

Whatever path you choose, try to keep a balance between work and play, but ultimately, make your work your play. Follow your joy and live fearlessly in your quest to fulfill your dreams. Speaking of which, we've touched upon the topic of fear previously, but let's revisit it once again because it can be your greatest enemy if you allow it to take over your thoughts and actions. It can put a halt to your progress, stopping you dead in your tracks.

When you reach outside of your comfort zone, it's inevitable you will face fears and self-doubt, but you can have fear without fear having you. You just need to learn how to notice and manage your thoughts. You can do this in many ways. The following techniques are the ones I'm most familiar with. You may also find them helpful.

Motivational speaker Zig Ziglar said, "F-E-A-R has two meanings: Forget everything and run or face everything and rise. The choice is yours." There are two ways to approach fear when it comes your way. You can try to ignore it and push it away or you can face it head on and embrace it. If you choose the former, it will constantly torment you and try to pull you down. It will lead you to poor decisions that will stifle your goals. Fear can lead you to self-sabotage and make you feel defeated.

On the other hand, if you acknowledge and envelop the fear, it can be useful in showing you exactly what is holding you back. Personally, I've always battled with stage fright. Why? My underlying fear was I wasn't good enough or talented enough. I was a perfectionist and didn't want to come across as flawed. My fears interfered with my auditions as anxiety took over my body. My hands shook, my breath was short, my mouth was dry, my heart raced, and worst of all, my vibrato got faster and I'd get pitchy because of the lack of breath.

After much introspection, I discovered that certain things in my past triggered my feelings of inadequacy or unworthiness. I feared what other people would think of me, which is why auditions always seemed more like Judgment Day. I knew I was going to be scrutinized and subconsciously didn't feel talented enough. The only auditions I did really well at were the ones where I was too excited to be fearful (like my first audition in NYC) or if I didn't care about the outcome.

Only after I accepted fear as part of the journey and turned the anxiety into excitement did I become mentally and physically prepared to face the opportunities before me. I stopped being so hard on myself and just accepted that all I could do was show up and be the best, most confident version of myself possible.

I also stopped comparing myself to other singers I heard at the auditions, and I realized all I could do was be me. I invite you to do the same. Try not to be your own worst critic and let go of the harsh self-judgment. If you're facing any type of fear or anxiety, take a deep breath, close your eyes, and change your thoughts. Use empowering self-talk with each inhale and exhale. For instance, on the inhale say, "I have what it takes to do this," and on the exhale say, "I release the fear." Make fear a part of your journey and befriend it. Realize it will never go away but you can choose how to handle it when it appears. Recognize it, release it, and replace it with a better thought. Napoleon Hill said, "Fears are nothing more than a state of mind."

Most fears are triggered by past experiences, self-doubt, or self-limiting beliefs. Something inside you taps into the false beliefs you have about yourself. They come from some kind of subconscious programming you picked up along the way, so take some time to ask yourself why you are afraid. Once you get to the root causes of your triggers, you won't feel like you're being sucked away by a powerful undertow dragging you into an ocean of anxiety. You'll feel more in control when fear pops up, and you'll be able to handle it more effectively by noticing it, interrupting the old thoughts, and reframing it with an empowering thought that aligns with your dreams.

You can never totally eliminate fear, but you can learn how to respond to it. Take Batman for instance. He was deathly afraid of bats from his childhood experience of being thrown down a well with bats flying above him, but we all know the outcome of that. He eventually turned his extreme fear of bats into an identity that struck fear into the hearts of criminals by becoming a bat himself. He faced his fear with bravery and courage instead of letting his traumatic experience haunt him his entire life.

Yes, Batman is fictional, but you get the point. We always have a choice about how we react to our circumstances. The goal is to replace fear with unstoppable confidence.

When you're about to take up something new and fear and self-doubt start entering your mind, face them head on and keep going! You need to become comfortable with the uncomfortable and take risks. It's a well-known fact that you can't move forward by walking in place. In 1981, a Narcotics Anonymous publication said, "The definition of insanity is doing the same thing over and over again, but expecting different results." Be courageous and show up in the world as your most confident, authentic self, and let whatever happens happen. Above all, stay peaceful and believe in yourself.

Another method to handle fear-based thoughts is a technique taught by Brave Thinking Institute founder Mary Morrissey. Instead of looking fear in the face when it happens, she suggests that when fear, worry, or self-doubt appear, make an appointment with it three days away. Simply acknowledge that these thoughts are present, but then take control of when you're going to address them. Write the date down in your calendar, and when that day comes, keep the appointment, and write down what the fear, worry, or doubt wanted to say to you. Then ask yourself if it's still a concern. Chances are, it's no longer an issue. This technique lets you delay fear-based thoughts and frees you from them. You've essentially put yourself in the driver's seat and asked your concerns to sit in the backseat.

Gabby Bernstein, author of *The Universe Has Your Back*, tweeted, "Putting our faith in love instead of fear begins transforming our experiences." She also advises, "When you choose to perceive love over fear, life begins to flow." When fear pops up, she suggests you say, "I turn my fear into faith. I choose to see this differently." There's that word "choose" again! As we discussed previously, you mold your life by every thought you think and every decision you make.

Think about one fear that is blocking you from being free to live your best life. Is it real, or are you imagining it? Do you realize you are creating the fear? It's just your perception of the experience and not the experience itself. Choose to love yourself instead of letting your fears get in the way. The power in you is bigger than your fears. Always lean on that when you feel like you're falling into the anxiety zone.

Another way to break through and handle your inner reactions to fear is to release your non-serving, negative inner chatter through daily meditation. As we've discussed previously, mindfulness meditation keeps you in the present moment and takes you out of your head. You learn how to surrender your anxieties to your Higher Self, which lightens your load. But for those who aren't meditators, let's talk about the scientific reasons behind the nature of fear and some practical ways to handle it.

According to behavior expert John Assaraf, whenever you experience major changes like finding a new job, leaving a broken relationship, starting a new business, or when there is real or imagined danger, the amygdala, the emotional response center in your brain, fires off neurochemicals like cortisol, epinephrine, or norepineph- rine, which cause emotions we call fear. Fear leads us to fight, freeze, or run away, but in each case, it stops us from being at our best.

Most of our fears are based on past experiences that created belief patterns in us. Our brain creates neural pathways whenever we're triggered by these unfounded fears and goes on automatic pilot. However, the brain can change, master new skills, store new memo- ries, and create new neural pathways so we can choose a different response to fear when we're triggered. This is called neuroplasticity, and it's the basis for a program Assaraf designed to create new neural pathways to replace the old automatic responses to triggers.

If your fear is debilitating, I recommend Assaraf's course, *Winning the Game of Fear*, which is a method for recognizing your fears and understanding why you have them. It teaches techniques for releas- ing fear, including a series of exercises to train your subconscious. Called *Innercises*, these exercises help eliminate the disempowering emotions that create fear. This technique is similar to cognitive be- havioral therapy where you take small action steps toward your fears so the fear gradually lessens and diminishes.

Your fear triggers will never go away, but you'll learn how to respond differently so fear doesn't get in your way. Just like in the old adage, you'll be able to "face the fear and do it anyway" because you'll be equipped with the internal tools to build a new neural pathway.

Jon Berghoff, cofounder of the XCHANGE Approach, covered the topic of fear on a Hal Elrod podcast. He said we can learn how to reduce fear by using mindfulness meditation, changing our thoughts, and reframing the things we fear by asking empowering questions about what it is we want to happen and what that would look like. These are rather powerful questions that prompt us to think about how we envision things in a positive way, so keep them handy when fear arises.

Ask yourself: What do I want to happen? What would that look like? What would that feel like?

Berghoff also suggests changing your physiology by taking care of your body through exercise, eating healthy foods, and staying hydrated. As we discussed earlier, keeping your body in great shape will lead to greater self-confidence, which is exactly what you need at your weakest moments.

Speaking of physicality, another method of reducing physical manifestations of fear is simply to *shake it off*. I mean that literally in the sense of physically moving your body. If you've ever been an audience member attending a live TV broadcast, you know there's usually someone who warms up the crowd beforehand and does their best to get people energized to raise the room's vibration. Movement is a proven and effective way to alter your emotions, so why not use it when you're afraid?

One last approach I'm aware of for working through fears and anxiety is called Tapping or EFT (Emotional Freedom Technique). It involves tapping specific points on the body, mostly on the head and upper torso, in a particular sequence. In Chinese medicine, the points of contact being tapped are the body's energy meridian points, believed to be areas of the body through which energy flows. According to Jack Canfield, "Tapping is an intensely powerful tool that can help you quickly get over your biggest fears and help achieve all of your goals." It's a process of tapping on nine acupressure points while you simultaneously imagine the experience stimulating your fear.

Before you begin doing the tapping, you'll need to focus on the one fear bothering you in the moment. In a detailed blog post, Canfield explains that the areas tapped are on the top of your head, the eyebrow, the side of the eye, under the eye, under the nose, the chin, the collarbone, under the arm, and the *karate chop* area on the heel of your hand. Step one is to focus on the fear you're feeling and give it a rating between one and ten, with one being the lowest and ten being the highest level of fear you're experiencing. This will give you a baseline for how intense the fear is.

Start by tapping the heel of your hand ten times while describing the fear out loud and how it's making you feel. Repeat that three times and really tune into the feeling.

Next, state the fear starting with the words, "Even though I have this fear of," and add an affirmation after, saying, "I deeply and completely love and accept myself." For example, "Even though I have this fear of being judged, I deeply and completely love and accept myself." You're going to recite this phrase while tapping each of the acupressure points, and then repeat the sequence two more times. When you're done, rate your level of fear from one to ten. By this time, your fear should have gone down, and you should be much calmer.

For more information on how to use EFT, check out the articles listed in the Resources section or google it. It's a popular tactic for not only facing fears but for treating all kinds of psychological issues.

Many people have found this method extremely helpful, so give it a whirl and see if it works for you.

Last but not least, there's an entire book called *Feel the Fear and Do It Anyway* by Susan Jeffers devoted entirely to this topic.

Now that you know there are ways to stay out of the debilitating fear zone, answer this question: What would you be doing if you weren't afraid? Take a moment to think about that.

Here are a few exercises to help you assimilate this chapter's content.

EXERCISE 1: DEFINING YOUR CURRENT JOB STATUS

This exercise will help you decipher whether your job is worth keeping or you need to start moving to something different. Take out your journal and write down any thoughts that come to mind when you ask yourself the following questions. The goal is to clarify your best plan of action, whether it means staying in or leaving your current situation.

1. Do you look forward to getting up in the morning and going to work?

2. Are your natural abilities and skills being used in a field that brings you joy?

3. Are you truly interested in your job?

4. Does your job give you flexibility to do the things you enjoy?

5. Is your job serving you or are you serving it?

6. Does your job light you up or are you merely working for a paycheck?

7. Is your job holding you back from your dreams?

8. What action steps can you take to move into your true calling?

To give yourself a boost, go to YouTube and check out Dolly Parton's parody of "9 to 5" called "5 to 9," which is featured on a Squarespace commercial. It will give you a visual about chasing your dreams while still working your day job. I've included the link in the Resources section.

EXERCISE 2: FACING YOUR FEARS

1. Get yourself in a comfy position in a chair.

2. Close your eyes and take a few deep breaths.

3. Pick one fear and mentally put yourself in that situation. Visualize it and feel it.

4. Notice how this fear physically affects your body. Where do you carry the tension? Do you experience tightness in your stomach or chest? A racing heart? Stomach butterflies? Wherever it's located, breathe into that area with deep breaths.

5. Ask yourself where this fear originated. Did something happen when you were younger? Did it make you feel like you weren't good enough? What story have you been feeding your subconscious about it? Is it true?

6. When you're experiencing this particular fear, become mindful of your thoughts. Take a few deep breaths and choose empowering self-talk with each inhale and exhale. For instance, if you're like me and get nervous before performing or public speaking, say to yourself, "I radiate confidence," and on the exhale, say, "I release all fear." Make up your own affirmations that you know will calm you down. Keep doing this and make it a habit to mentally rehearse facing your specific fears. Visualize what you want your outcome to be.

You get to choose whether you let your fear get the best of you or create new techniques to work around them. If fear is an issue, try some of the methods to see what works best for you.

In the next chapter, I'll pass on a few more words of inspiration to keep you focused on living the dream life of your own creation and show you how there are lessons to be learned all around you when you remain mindful of your surroundings.

CHAPTER 13

YOU'RE IN THE SPOTLIGHT!

*"All the world's a stage, and all the men
and women merely players."*

— William Shakespeare

Yes, life is a stage, and you are the star in your own grand production. No matter what profession you're in, what relationships you're in, or what piques your interest, you get to choose your character, write your own script, and direct your own show. No masks are required in your own original production because this is your chance to let your authentic self shine! Try not to live your life as a character in someone else's play. If you've made it this far in the book, you know better and wouldn't dare do that to yourself. You are a unique masterpiece and have your own special gifts to bring to the world. Stay on target with what you're here to do.

You're also now aware that your inner director has the most glorious vision for you, so keep looking inward for direction. Let the whispers from your soul take center stage to guide you to your most fulfilling life. Your Higher Self knows the real reason you're here and what's in your best interest. Trust it. We're all here on purpose, for a purpose.

If you're just starting out on your career path, my advice is to stick with it if you absolutely love what you're doing. Everyone faces challenges and hurdles, but these tend to make you more knowledgeable and marketable as long as you pay attention to what you're supposed to be learning. If you've left your dreams behind for a mediocre, non-fulfilling life that just puts food on the table, I get it, but it doesn't have to stay that way. If you have a dream in your heart, it's calling for you to make it happen. You came out of the womb with the divine right to live a rich and fulfilling life, despite the circumstances you were born into. You deserve to have it all, but to get there, you must follow your joy and passions.

If you're familiar with Joseph Campbell's book *The Hero's Journey*, you'll recognize it's very much a parallel to what seems to be happening to you in this very moment. In Campbell's book, the main character leaves his ordinary life to go on an adventure. He faces trials and challenges along the way but returns home victorious. Similarly, you are starting out from your normal, everyday life and feel called to do something greater. You feel a deep yearning to do more than what you're doing now. You're opening up your mind to doing things differently, and you're ready to embark on a new venture despite your fear of the unknown. You're committing yourself to following your calling and connecting to your deeper purpose. You're letting go of your old, non-serving thought patterns and creating new, powerful ones. You're learning and absorbing new, helpful ways to be your best self, and you're sharing your wisdom with others. Your life is transforming into something greater than you could have ever imagined. You are indeed the hero in your own life!

It's very easy to let our comfortable lives remain as is, which is fine if you're not feeling a longing to do something else. However, if you want to make a change, you need to train yourself to become comfortable with being uncomfortable. No matter what, stay focused on your bigger vision and take small steps every day to make it happen. Incorporate the principles mentioned in this book that resonate with you into your everyday life. Keep meditating, doing your affirmations and visualizations, and remember that what you can conceive and believe, you will achieve. With each thought, decision, and action, you're creating the screenplay of your life. Every day starts out with a fresh new blank page to fill up as you choose, so bring all the good stuff in that makes you happy. Yes, you get to dream your own dream and make it your reality.

One of the founders of the Human Potential Movement, Dr. Jean Houston, has very eloquently defined and summed up our time here on Earth as the *art of becoming*. We're always changing, growing, and evolving. Our dreams may change as we change, but whatever it is you wish to do now, go for it with enthusiasm, courage, and determination—and don't let anything get in your way or stop you from pursuing the life you crave.

> *"It's never too late to be who you might have been."*
>
> — *George Eliot*

Not to be morbid, but none of us will be on this planet in 200 years. We don't know when, but there's no escaping our mortality. When we're young and vital, we don't think about this and avoid the topic altogether. We tend to live in the here and now while planning for our future, but at the same time, we neglect thinking about living a purposeful life filled with passion, intention, and contribution. We don't realize our innate talents are to be used both for our own advancement and to serve the world in our unique way. We believe what we see in the outside world is all there is. Most people don't delve into their spiritual nature to find they're not just their physical body. And most public schools don't teach about spirituality because this topic is too related to religion. My first-grade teacher asked us to close our eyes and then slowly asked us to tune into our five senses by asking what we heard, felt, tasted, smelled, and saw. It was essentially my first mindfulness meditation, so maybe this teacher knew more than she was allowed to teach.

I'd like to take on the role of teacher right now and give you a *life homework assignment*. While you're busy going after your dreams, I'd like you to learn to practice the mind-body-soul connection within the course of your day. Live with the intention of having more peace, love, and joy in your life, but *be* the peace, love, and joy as you walk this Earth. Radiate compassion and heart toward everyone you meet. Use your life to grow, evolve, and have fun, while at the same time, helping others along the way to do the same. Let the world benefit from the life you've led. We were born to make the most of the time we have on Earth, so take advantage of each precious breath you take. Also, don't let your age discourage you from doing what you love. If you take care of your body, keep your brain sharp, and stay spiritually connected, there's no reason you can't stay vital and radiant until your time is up.

I'm incredibly inspired by stories of seniors in their eighties, nineties, and even hundreds continuing to live active and fulfilling lives. I had the honor of meeting one of them in 2017. Tae Porchon-Lynch was the oldest yoga teacher in the world. Born in India, she had an immediate love for yoga, and it became her life-long practice. She taught yoga for more than ninety years and was an award-winning author. At the age of eighty-seven, she decided to take on ballroom dancing and ended up winning more than 700 competitions!

I took one of her yoga classes and, although she had an assistant for the difficult moves, her strength and flexibility were incredibly intact. She also gave each of us individual attention on our form and demonstrated the poses if we were doing them wrong. When she came over to me, her little tweaks to my body were difficult to manage. This ninety-eight-year-old woman was kicking my butt! During the classes, she also shared words of wisdom like, "Nothing is impossible" and "Age is just a number." My favorite quote of hers was, "When I wake up in the morning, I look at the sun, and I say, 'This is going to be the best day of my life,' and it will be. It always is." She died peacefully in 2020 at the age of 101—she taught until a few days before her death. She's my hero, and I hope her story inspires you to keep going too.

"Do anything, but let it produce joy."

— Walt Whitman

One of my dear friends commented that my book is the song I was always meant to sing. He was so right. Everything that happened in my life shaped me into the person I am today and allowed me to share my story with others. We all have our own original songs emanating from our stories. Each of us has a chance to get stronger when we encounter obstacles on our path and learn the best routes around them to get where we want to be. We are intrinsically more than our circumstances and so much stronger than we think we are. So, keep in mind that any problems we encounter aren't permanent, and choose to take this journey in peace, grace, and ease. Trust your inner voice; trust life; above all, never give up on yourself or your dreams!

Most likely, you're familiar with Frank Sinatra's song "My Way" in which he expresses how he lived his life under his own terms. It's now time for you to do it *your way!* With the tools and concepts in this book, you have the means to fast-track your life in a calm, controlled, and peaceful way. You know it's in your best interest to create new daily habits that serve you so you can make progress toward your goals. You're now aware that you have control over your thoughts, and that thoughts can be changed. You know you need to take action steps in the direction of your desired life. You also know you don't have control over outcomes, and it's in your best interest to go-with-the-flow instead of resisting what's happening. Hopefully, you've discovered the spiritual side of yourself and know you can always turn within to find guidance, strength, comfort, and ultimately, everything you need to power up your life.

One of my favorite poems is "Desiderata." I discovered this treasure in the 1990s, and I refer to it in times of stress. Being that my life has been rather peaceful over the past few years, I hadn't looked at it in quite a long time, but I recently took a gander at it only to discover that it very eloquently summarizes many of the topics discussed in this book, starting with the line, "Go placidly amid the noise and the haste, and remember what peace there may be in silence," and offering the advice to, "be cheerful, be happy, and keep peace in your soul." I didn't realize this one-page poem had so much influence on my life. I suggest you take a look at it to see if it resonates with you. You can find it in the back of this book.

"I have lived with several Zen masters—all of them cats."

— Eckhart Tolle

For a lighthearted change of pace, I'd like to convey some life lessons I've learned from all of the furry cats I've lived with throughout my life. Animals have no pretenses and are born knowing exactly what they're here to do, so I think we can learn a thing or two from our pets. Here's what I noticed:

- They're fearless and bold and don't care what other animals think of them.

- They live in the moment.

- They don't judge, and they don't hold grudges. They automatically know how to let things slide and move on.

- They love unconditionally and forgive easily.

- They're persistent in getting what they want. If they need to go outside, they won't stop trying to get your attention until you open the door or take them out. And they definitely let you know when they're hungry!

- They ask for what they want and aren't apologetic for being needy.

- They always feel deserving of their happiest life.

- They trust their instincts at all times.

- They are who they are, and they can do nothing other than be themselves.

So, the next time you play with your pet, keep in mind that aside from the love and joy they bring into your life, they come equipped to share their wisdom with you.

Not only can we learn from animals, but we can also find hidden lessons in nature. Take a walk outside and look around. Every plant, tree, insect, bird, and living thing has its own internal intelligence keeping it alive. They don't have to do anything but be what they were created to be. If you're like most people, you don't usually take the time to think about how fascinating our planet is, but it's truly magical once you become mindful of your surroundings. Have you ever watched science documentaries where they film all the different types of sea creatures? Have you ever seen a squid or octopus turn invisible? They can do that to protect themselves from predators. How amazing is that?

I encourage you to remain curious about your environment and marvel at its wonders. *You* are a huge part of the magic, and all you have to do is be yourself and let yourself light up the world.

Our time together is almost up, so let's move on to the conclusion since I have a few more words of motivational inspiration for you. Turn the page if you're ready.

CONCLUSION

IT'S A WRAP!

When all the scenes of a movie have been shot or a show comes to an end, the final proclamation from the director is, "It's a wrap!" Since it's time for our parting words, I'd like to congratulate you for sticking with me throughout this book. Celebrate yourself for showing up and being open to finding new ways to elevate yourself to your highest vision! I sincerely hope you'll take some of the tidbits of advice and use the tools, habits, and concepts we've discussed to enhance your life and boldly move forward toward your desired Point B. I'd like to commend you for making the commitment to yourself to become all you can be without limitations and live the life you love living. If we were face-to-face, I'd give you a big hug!

Let's review and affirm what you've learned. Here's a list of empowering statements to carry throughout your days. Take a moment to deeply absorb them into your psyche. Breathe them into your body and soul because this, my fellow being, is your new truth and way of living.

- You're worth it.

- You matter.

- Your life matters.

- You deserve to have your best life.

- You are a unique expression in this world.

- Everything you need is inside of you.

- Be kind and gentle with yourself.

- Be mindful of your thoughts and make empowering decisions.

- Trust in your gut instincts.

- Detach from outcomes.

- Live fearlessly.

- Hone your craft.

- Don't compare yourself to others.

- Surround yourself with positive, uplifting people.

- Choose your thoughts wisely.

- Know that the answers to all your questions lie within.

- Tap into your spiritual nature daily.

- Develop productive morning habits.

- Focus on what you want and not what you don't want.

- Face your fears and show up confidently.

- Live in peace.

- Love, honor, and respect yourself and your precious life.

- Have a joyful mind.

- Visualize your ideal life and feel what that feels like.

- Never give up on yourself or your dreams!

And to reinforce what you just read, let's make it a little more personal. I'd like you to read each of the following affirmations out loud and *feel* every bit of them. To make it even more effective, record yourself saying them and listen to it every day to feed your subconscious your new truths. To make it even more effectual, do it while looking at yourself in the mirror. You've got this. Ready? Stand in your superpower pose and let's go!

- I am worth it!

- I matter!

- My life matters!

- I am deserving of my best life!

- I am a unique expression in this world!

- Everything I need is inside of me!

- I am kind and gentle with myself.

- I am mindful of my thoughts and make empowering decisions.

- I trust my gut instincts.

- I detach from outcomes.

- I live fearlessly!

- I take time to hone my craft.

- I don't compare myself to others.

- I surround myself with positive, uplifting people.

- I choose my thoughts wisely.

- I know the answers to all my questions lie within.

- I tap into my spiritual nature daily.

- I am developing productive morning habits.

- I focus on what I want and not what I don't want.

- I face my fears and show up confidently.

- I always choose to be at peace.

- I love, honor, and respect myself and my precious life.

- I have a joyful mind.

- I envision my ideal life and embrace how amazing it feels!

- I will never give up on myself or my dreams!

Yes, yes, yes! You are every bit of this! Even though you might have gotten off to a rough start, there's no reason to stay there. You have a choice whether to stay stuck in the lower energies of depression, anxiety, frustration, guilt, shame, or anger, or choose to raise your vibration to all the better feelings—love, peace, and joy. You have the power to choose and create your own magnificent story. Keep journaling, and develop new empowering habits, including the M&Ms of **M**orning Rituals, **M**editation, **M**indfulness, **M**ovement, **M**usic, and appreciating how **M**agical life is. Keep a bag of M&Ms nearby as a reminder.

Start trusting that all is going well in your world, even if things appear otherwise. Life is always working on your behalf, so live fearlessly and push yourself to leave your comfort zone. Challenge yourself. Take risks. Become comfortable with the uncomfortable and be open to new opportunities to learn, grow, and expand into your highest self.

Always keep in mind that there's no final destination. It's all about the journey, the experiences, the lessons, the growth, the discovery, and the joy of life. Expect the unexpected, embrace every achievement, and embrace every challenge because challenges make you stronger. Commit to always staying true to being your most authentic, beautiful self.

Imagine waking up every morning excited to start out the day doing what you love and knowing that your life has meaning. Stay inspired by listening to podcasts, reading books, and subscribing to daily newsletters that motivate you and help you on your journey. As I was writing this book, a new app came onto the scene called Clubhouse where you can listen to your favorite speakers and choose topics of interest. You can even create your own *room* and hold your own talks. This is yet another way to surround yourself with positive, supportive, non-judgmental people who will encourage you to keep going.

Always live with an attitude of gratitude because you'll keep attracting more and more things to be grateful about.

Achieving your dreams takes perseverance and an unwavering belief that you deserve to have an abundant, fulfilling life that includes your passions. I know you have what it takes by the mere fact that you've read this whole book. You're more than ready for the never-ending voyage of becoming the best possible version of yourself. You're not here merely to exist; you're here to thrive, so keep going and keep growing. Once your life starts to shift and transform, people will begin to notice the change in you, and you'll be an inspiration to them to start living their best lives. You'll be a blessing to everyone you meet just by being you.

As Henry David Thoreau said, "Go confidently in the direction of your dreams!" And Confucius advises, "It does not matter how slowly you go, as long as you do not stop." It's time for you to shine, my friend. You no longer have to be a background player in someone else's movie. The spotlight is all yours, and the world is ready to receive your gifts.

Now that you own all the magnificence of who you are, your life is going to climb to new heights. With much love, I wish you a beautiful journey. Live in peace and joy, believe in yourself, and never give up on what your heart is calling you to do.

Cheers to you—the best is yet to come!

DESIDERATA

GO PLACIDLY amid the noise and the haste, and remember what peace there may be in silence. As far as possible, without surrender, be on good terms with all persons.

Speak your truth quietly and clearly; and listen to others, even to the dull and the ignorant; they too have their story.

Avoid loud and aggressive persons; they are vexatious to the spirit. If you compare yourself with others, you may become vain or bitter, for always there will be greater and lesser persons than yourself.

Enjoy your achievements as well as your plans. Keep interested in your own career, however humble; it is a real possession in the changing fortunes of time.

Exercise caution in your business affairs, for the world is full of trickery. But let this not blind you to what virtue there is; many persons strive for high ideals, and everywhere life is full of heroism.

Be yourself. Especially do not feign affection. Neither be cynical about love; for in the face of all aridity and disenchantment, it is as perennial as the grass.

Take kindly the counsel of the years, gracefully surrendering the things of youth.

Nurture strength of spirit to shield you in sudden misfortune. But do not distress yourself with dark imaginings. Many fears are born of fatigue and loneliness.

Beyond a wholesome discipline, be gentle with yourself. You are a child of the universe no less than the trees and the stars; you have a right to be here.

And whether or not it is clear to you, no doubt the universe is unfolding as it should. Therefore be at peace with God, whatever you conceive Him to be. And whatever your labors and aspirations, in the noisy confusion of life, keep peace in your soul. With all its sham, drudgery and broken dreams, it is still a beautiful world. Be cheerful. Strive to be happy.

— Max Ehrmann, 1927

ACKNOWLEDGMENTS

A heartfelt thank you to all the people who have enhanced my life with unconditional love, joy, and laughter. To my adorable, supportive husband, Jim, who has kept me sane and balanced throughout this writing journey and who has been a gift in my life ever since we met one fateful day on 42nd Street in New York City on a Match.com date.

To my brother and sister, David and Marlene, who lived through the turmoil of our upbringing and sustained the same internal injuries but somehow managed to find their way back to themselves.

To my beautiful nieces and nephews, Matt, Faith, Tom, Ginny, and Will, whom I've watched grow up to be outstanding humans, staying true to their callings, breaking the chain of dysfunction, and raising their own children in a space of pure love.

Huge gratitude to my book coach, Christine Gail—without her guidance and expertise, this book would not have been written in such a timely fashion.

To my book coaching accountability partners, Renée Marino and Lorraine Thomson, who were always there to support, encourage, and inspire me throughout our mutual writing journeys together.

To my awesomely fun Manhattan Plaza friends who have inspired me with their own creative talents and dreams and who brought me so much loving support when I needed it the most.

To my close childhood friends and high school buddies who unknowingly kept me holding on to the will to live during my challenging times.

To my sweet friend Lynda who has carried and supported me through my rollercoaster life without judgment.

To all my singer and musician friends in the numerous bands and groups I've been in over the years who have pushed me to be better at my craft by sharing and shining their musical genius in my presence. A special thank you to the heartwarming sisterhood of the Belle Tones and to the creative band members of The 80's Revolution Band who constantly keep me on my professional toes.

To my mother and father who left us early in life. I know they did the best they could. All I have for them is love because if it weren't for my turbulent childhood, I wouldn't be who I am today.

To my cousins Lenny, Ruth, and Marc, who endured the same type of childhood neglect; thank you for being so open to sharing your perspectives from your own challenges.

To my cousins Gail, Jamie, Ashley, and Paula, you all inspired me as a writer because of your own natural flair for putting pen to paper.

To my cousins Phyllis and Marvin, your welcoming visits and family knowledge have been a treasure.

And to my closest-in-age-cousin Howie, you inspire me by staying true to your own unique calling in Israel and for the warmth I feel from your supportive messages.

To my friends Wilfredo and Miriam who have provided years of interesting dinner conversations and who are adored for their loving and supportive ways.

To my muses Lisa Spinelli, Robyn Triolo Caruso, and Phil Shimmel who encouraged and inspired me to write a book.

To all of the people in my past who have unknowingly helped shape me into the woman I am today.

And finally, thank you to the countless friends and acquaintances who have helped make my journey through life more colorful, fun, and exciting. You have been the spice in my life, and I envelop you in gratitude and love.

RESOURCES

The following are links to the many teachers, mentors, creative artists, and motivational speakers mentioned throughout this book.

Andrea Sooch, Actress
www.andreasooch.net

Betsy Finkelhoo, Author of *Power Affirmation Journal*
www.finkelhoo.com

Billy Gilman, Singer & Recording Artist
www.billygilman.com

Christine Gail, Author of *Unleash Your Rising*
www.UnleashYourRising.com

Denna Babul, Author of *The Fatherless Daughter Project*
www.dennababul.com

Dolly Parton, Legendary Singer
www.dollyparton.com
Remake of her song "9 to 5" called "5 to 9"
Short version: www.youtube.com/watch?v=v4FYL8twE6Q
Long version: www.youtube.com/watch?v=y8jF96hoF9M

Emily Fletcher, Founder of *Ziva Meditation* & the M-Word technique
www.zivameditation.com

Erin Stutland, Author of *Mantras In Motion*
www.erinstutland.com

Hal Elrod, Author of *The Miracle Morning*
www.halelrod.com & www.miraclemorning.com

Jack Canfield, Author of *The Success Principles*
www.jackcanfield.com

John Assaraf, Author of *Innercise*
www.johnassaraf.com

Lewis Howes, Creator of *The School of Greatness* podcast
www.lewishowes.com

Marisa Corvo, Singer & Recording Artist
www.marisacorvomusic.com

Mary Morrissey, Founder of *Brave Thinking Institute*
www.marymorrissey.com
www.bravethinkinginstitute.com

Mike Dooley, Creator of *Notes from The Universe*
www.tut.com

Stig Severinsen, Author of *Breatheology*
www.breatheology.com

Vishen Lakhiani, Founder & CEO of Mindvalley
www.mindvalley.com
3 Questions YouTube video:
www.youtube.com/watch?v=f8eU5Pc-y0g

Further Recommended Reading

Building Your Field of Dreams (1997)
by Mary Manin Morrissey

*Healing the Child Within: Discovery and Recovery for
Adult Children of Dysfunctional Families* (1987)
by Charles L. Whitfield

Inner Bonding: Becoming a Loving Adult to Your Inner Child (1992)
by Margaret Paul

*The Map of Consciousness Explained: A Proven Energy Scale
to Actualize Your Ultimate Potential* (2020)
by David R. Hawkins

*Raise Your Vibration: 111 Practices to Increase
Your Spiritual Connection* (2016)
by Kyle Gray

The Universe Has Your Back: Transform Fear to Faith (2018)
by Gabby Bernstein

Unleash Your Rising: Lead with Intention and Ignite Your Story (2019)
by Christine Gail

10 Secrets for Success and Inner Peace (2016)
by Dr. Wayne W. Dyer

END NOTES

INTRODUCTION

https://capitalistcreations.com/youve-got-some-looming-childhood-issues/

CHAPTER 3

https://www.pressconnects.com/story/news/local/2019/03/18/ask-scientist-how-do-thoughts-work-our-brain/3153303002/

https://eric.ed.gov/?id=EJ1155571

https://www.healyourlife.com/do-you-make-a-difference

https://www.youtube.com/watch?v=0JHVVyPcRmg; https://innerself.com/content/personal/happiness-and-self-help/4879-authentic-wisdom.htm

https://www.collective-evolution.com/2014/09/27/this-is-the-world-of-quantum-physics-nothing-is-solid-and-everything-is-energy/

https://www.britannica.com/biography/Nikola-Tesla; https://en.wikipedia.org/wiki/Nikola_Tesla

https://ed.ted.com/lessons/brian-greene-on-string-theory

CHAPTER 4

https://en.wikipedia.org/wiki/Émile_Coué

https://www.psychologicalscience.org/news/releases/smiling-facilitates-stress-recovery.html

https://thework.com/instruction-the-work-byron-katie/

CHAPTER 5

https://blog.dce.harvard.edu/professional-development/3-ways-boost-productivity-morning-ritual

https://www.bravethinkinginstitute.com/blog/life-transformation/5-ways-to-have-your-best-day-ever

https://spacioustherapy.com/brain-changes-improves-mindfulness-interventions-meditation/; https://www.ncbi.nlm.nih.gov/pmc/articles/PMC3345952/

https://www.thecut.com/2019/05/i-now-suspect-the-vagus-nerve-is-the-key-to-well-being.html

https://www.healthline.com/nutrition/12-benefits-of-meditation#10.-Helps-control-pain

https://www.washingtonpost.com/news/inspired-life/wp/2015/05/26/harvard-neuroscientist-meditation-not-only-reduces-stress-it-literally-changes-your-brain/

https://mindworks.org/blog/how-meditation-changes-the-brain/

http://www.ijahss.com/Paper/05102020/1179451276.pdf

https://centrespringmd.com/docs/How%20Habits%20are%20Formed.pdf

CHAPTER 6

https://www.countryliving.com/life/a35953/savers-morning-routine/

https://www.ncbi.nlm.nih.gov/pmc/articles/PMC3734071/

https://pubmed.ncbi.nlm.nih.gov/10052073/

https://pubmed.ncbi.nlm.nih.gov/25167363/

https://neurosciencenews.com/musicians-brain-connections-17611/

https://www.ucf.edu/pegasus/your-brain-on-music/

https://www.youtube.com/watch?v=-_xf8WpvUA4

https://www.apa.org/monitor/2013/11/music

Music Therapy Findings:

Premature babies: https://pathways.org/music-to-their-ears-how-music-therapy-benefits-premature-babies-in-the-nicu/

Depression: https://www.healthypeople.gov/2020/tools-resources/evidence-based-resource/music-therapy-for-depression

Parkinson's: https://www.apdaparkinson.org/article/music-therapy-parkinsons-disease/

https://www.health.harvard.edu/blog/nutritional-psychiatry-your-brain-on-food-201511168626

CHAPTER 7

https://en.wikipedia.org/wiki/Law_of_attraction_(New_Thought)

https://www.drwaynedyer.com/blog/manifesting-your-desires/

https://www.developgoodhabits.com/online-vision-board/

https://twitter.com/marymorrissey/status/1241814544864985090; https://www.youtube.com/watch?v=1fHl2CS33a4

https://www.marymorrissey.com/blog/shifting-your-vibration-by-mary-morrissey/

https://m.facebook.com/marymaninmorrissey/photos/a.21050685 2315349/4148482381851090/?type=3

https://en.wikipedia.org/wiki/Don%27t_Worry,_Be_Happy# Certifications%20Chapter%2012:

https://www.facebook.com/watch/?v=1201680506531307

https://www.fearlessmotivation.com/2018/09/27/overcome-any-fear-john-assaraf/

https://halelrod.com/4-proven-ways-to-breakthrough-your-fears/

https://www.medicalnewstoday.com/articles/326434#overview

https://www.jackcanfield.com/blog/tapping-therapy/

https://www.healthline.com/health/eft-tapping#treatment

ABOUT THE AUTHOR

Gloria Carpenter is a certified Dreambuilder life coach, motivational speaker and a professional singer in the New York area. Her background in theater and dance shines through in her performances, exuding a bright and vivacious presence whenever she steps on stage. She has given thousands of performances over the years working on cruise ships, in cover bands, orchestras, jazz trios, tribute acts, and country bands, and she has also appeared and recorded with many original projects. Gloria has teamed with numerous world class musicians and has opened for name acts like Billy Gilman, Frankie Valli, and Micky Dolenz of the Monkees. She has always been driven to live a life she loves, which is why she is quick to encourage others to live the life of their dreams.

Gloria's mission is to see people happy and fulfilled doing what they love by utilizing their innate talents. Coming from a childhood of neglect and abandonment, she knows all too well how inner wounds can cause people to get stuck in their tracks by their disempowering thoughts and actions. In her new book, *Power Up Your Dreams*, she shares what it takes to stay true to your own unique path with uplifting words of wisdom and guidance to help you achieve your deepest desires!

WORK WITH GLORIA!

Are you inspired to take action in pursuit of your dream life?

If the concepts and practices within this book resonated with you and you'd like to take it one step further and apply them to your life with coaching and accountability, Gloria would love to work with you. She is a certified Dreambuilder Life Coach through the Brave Thinking Institute. She can help you design and create a life in harmony with your soul's purpose.

If you're looking to gain clarity and confidence and achieve your next level of success while enjoying the highest levels of fulfillment in life, Gloria's coaching programs can help you get there.

For a free consultation or to learn more, visit:
www.PowerUpYourDreams.com

Made in the USA
Middletown, DE
27 November 2021

53006893R00137